TITANS OF TRADE AND POWER: THE RUTHLESS RISE AND DOMINATION OF HISTORY'S GREATEST LEADERS

ADEEB JAMAL

This book is dedicated to the visionaries who dared to dream beyond the horizon, the pioneers whose boundless ambition and resilience forged empires that changed the world, and the leaders who, in pursuit of their visions, reshaped industries, economies, and societies. Your stories remind us that innovation comes not just from brilliance, but from an unwavering commitment to see through challenges and defy the odds.

To the countless men and women whose names may not be remembered, yet whose contributions laid the foundations for progress, this work honors your unsung efforts.

To my family, who have been my compass and my constant source of strength, thank you for your patience, love, and unyielding belief in me. Your support has been the cornerstone of every endeavor I have taken on, and your wisdom has guided me through both my brightest and most trying moments.

To my mentors and educators who have instilled in me the values of curiosity, hard work, and integrity, your teachings have left an indelible mark on my journey and will forever shape my path forward. This book would not have been possible without the inspiration and insight you imparted.

And finally, to aspiring entrepreneurs, thinkers, and leaders around the world: may this book serve as a testament to the power of vision, the necessity of resilience, and the importance of learning from those who came before. May you find in these pages the motivation to pursue your own ambitions with unwavering determination.

— Adeeb Jamal (Author)

Contents

Foreword

When Adeeb Jamal first shared with me his vision for this book, I knew immediately that it was the beginning of something special. As his mentor and teacher, I have watched him grow from a curious, ambitious student into an individual with a deep passion for understanding the intricacies of business history and the strategies that shape our world. To see him channel that passion into this comprehensive work at the young age of 17 is both inspiring and a testament to his remarkable dedication and talent.

This book, Titans of Trade and Power: The Relentless Pursuit and Dominance of History's Greatest Business Leaders, is not just a collection of biographies; it is an insightful analysis of the principles, successes, and failures that have defined the paths of the greatest business minds throughout history. Adeeb dives into the human stories behind the brands, technologies, and industries that have shaped our world.

What sets Adeeb apart is his ability to connect historical context with present-day implications. He understands that the lessons from Rockefeller's iron grip on the oil industry or Walt Disney's visionary storytelling do not exist in a vacuum—they resonate with today's leaders and aspiring entrepreneurs alike. Adeeb's ability to draw these connections reflects his keen intellect and relentless pursuit of knowledge, qualities that any teacher would be proud to witness.

This book's structure is particularly compelling. Each chapter delves into the three critical stages of these leaders' journeys: their beginnings, their peak achievements, and their legacy as it stands today. This format not only provides a narrative arc that is easy to follow but also delivers valuable lessons that emerge from the complexities of their paths—lessons that remind us of the importance of innovation, resilience, and ethical decision-making.

As you read through the stories of these business titans, I encourage you to appreciate the diligence and dedication that Adeeb has poured into every page. He has spent countless hours researching, writing, and refining this book, driven by the same spirit of curiosity and tenacity that he so admires in the leaders he writes about. In a way, Adeeb's journey in creating this book mirrors the very stories it tells: a young individual facing challenges, learning from them, and emerging with a finished work that reflects both ambition and insight.

For young readers, this book is a reminder that age is never a barrier to pursuing your dreams. For seasoned business professionals, it offers fresh perspectives on familiar stories and invites reflection on how the past can inform future strategies. And for anyone with an interest in the power of human ambition, this book is a compelling read that captures the essence of what it takes to build something that endures.

It is an honor to write this foreword and an even greater privilege to have played a part in Adeeb's journey. I have no doubt that this book is only the beginning of what he will achieve.

— Aanadi Kirti Pratap
(Mentor and Teacher of Adeeb Jamal)

Preface

The idea for Titans of Trade and Power: The Relentless Pursuit and Dominance of History's Greatest Business Leaders was born out of my deep fascination with the forces that drive human ambition and the strategies that propel some individuals to create legacies that endure through generations. The answer to what inspired me to embark on the challenge of writing a book of this scale is both simple and complex: a deep-seated desire to understand what makes a true leader and the lessons we can draw from those who dared to challenge the status quo.

The journey of creating this book has been as enlightening as it has been demanding. I delved into historical archives, pored over biographies, and analyzed countless interviews and documentaries to capture the essence of these figures. It wasn't just about recounting facts but about telling the human stories that lie beneath the business empires. Each of these leaders—be it Henry Ford, who brought automobiles to the masses, or Steve Jobs, who changed how we interact with technology—demonstrated a level of vision and tenacity that set them apart. This book seeks to reveal not just what they achieved, but how and why they did it.

The structure of this book is designed to take the reader through three pivotal stages in the lives of these leaders: their formative years and the challenges they faced, the peak of their influence and the strategies that defined their leadership, and finally, the lasting impact they left behind. This approach allows for a nuanced understanding of how their early experiences shaped their philosophies and how their decisions resonated far beyond their time.

One of the central themes you will find throughout these pages is the delicate balance between ambition and ethics. Figures like John D. Rockefeller and Andrew Carnegie were titans of their time, driving the industrial engine that powered nations. Yet, their legacies are marked by debates over the power of monopolies, wealth distribution, and social responsibility. I wanted to confront these complexities head-on to present a balanced view that acknowledges both their monumental achievements and the criticisms they faced.

The stories of these leaders are not just business lessons; they are studies in human resilience, creativity, and the relentless pursuit of something greater than oneself.

Writing this book has been more than an academic exercise; it has been a personal journey of growth and understanding. I've come to realize that the essence of leadership lies in the ability to navigate failure, to pivot when circumstances change, and to remain steadfast in the face of adversity. The stories within these chapters are filled with moments of triumph, yes, but also with moments of doubt, miscalculation, and recalibration. For every success, there was a risk taken, a lesson learned, and a decision that shaped the future.

I owe a great deal of gratitude to the mentors and teachers who have fueled my passion for learning and guided me along this path, especially Aanadi Kirti Pratap, whose wisdom and encouragement have been invaluable. To my family, your unwavering support has given me the strength to take on challenges that seemed insurmountable. And to my readers, I hope this book ignites your curiosity and inspires you to look beyond the surface of success, to understand the layers of determination, strategy, and vision that create true titans of industry.

In closing, my greatest hope for this book is that it serves as both a source of inspiration and a reminder that greatness is not achieved overnight. It is built through perseverance, continuous learning, and the willingness to take bold steps. Whether you are a student, an aspiring entrepreneur, or simply someone intrigued by the stories of extraordinary individuals, may these pages remind you that within every leader's journey lies a story that is both unique and universal.

Acknowledgements

The journey of creating this book has been one of profound personal growth, intellectual challenge, and immense gratitude. It would not have been possible without the support and guidance of a number of exceptional individuals whose contributions, both direct and indirect, have shaped the content and structure of Titans of Trade and Power.

First and foremost, I must extend my deepest gratitude to Aanadi Kirti Pratap, my personal mentor and teacher, whose unwavering belief in my potential has been a constant source of motivation throughout this process. His wisdom, guidance, and encouragement have not only helped me refine my understanding of business history but have also nurtured my growth as a writer and thinker. His mentorship has been invaluable, and his insights have helped me stay focused and inspired, even during the most challenging stages of this project.

I also owe a great deal to the teachers and professors who have shaped my academic journey. Your dedication to fostering curiosity and critical thinking has laid the foundation for my understanding of the world of business, economics, and leadership. Each of you has imparted lessons that extended far beyond textbooks, teaching me how to approach problems with a strategic mindset, evaluate complex situations, and recognize the value of diverse perspectives.

A special thanks goes to my family, whose love and support have been the cornerstone of this book. To my parents, thank you for your unwavering belief in my abilities and for encouraging me to pursue my dreams, no matter how ambitious they may have seemed. Your constant support, both emotionally and practically, has made this endeavor possible. To my siblings, thank you for your patience, understanding, and for always being there to provide a sense of balance when the journey became overwhelming.

I would also like to express my appreciation to the biographers, historians, and authors whose works have served as the foundation for much of my research. Without the meticulous research and insightful analysis you have contributed to the public discourse on these historical figures, this book would not have been possible. I owe a great deal to your scholarship for providing the material and inspiration to tell these important stories.

To my friends, who have been sounding boards for my ideas and provided much-needed breaks during moments of stress, thank you for your friendship, encouragement, and perspective. You have been an essential part of this journey, and I am incredibly grateful for the time and energy you have invested in listening to my thoughts and ideas, offering advice, and sharing your own wisdom.

I must also acknowledge the team at Notion Press, whose professionalism and commitment to excellence in publishing have been crucial in bringing this book to life. From the editorial team to the designers, your efforts in ensuring that this book is polished and presentable have not gone unnoticed, and I am immensely grateful for your support and dedication.

Finally, I want to extend my heartfelt thanks to you, the reader. It is your curiosity, interest, and desire for knowledge that inspired this book to exist. It is my hope that these stories of remarkable individuals—of their rise, their challenges, and their lasting legacies—will resonate with you and inspire you in your own pursuits, whatever they may be. This book is as much yours as it is mine, and I am grateful that you have chosen to engage with it.

In conclusion, the writing of this book has been a collaborative effort in many ways, and I am deeply thankful to each and every one of you who has played a role, however large or small, in making Titans of Trade and Power a reality. Your encouragement, wisdom, and support have made this journey not only possible but also incredibly rewarding.

With deepest gratitude,
— Adeeb Jamal (author)

Prologue

In the fast-paced world of business and industry, a few remarkable individuals have left an indelible mark on history. They are the architects of the modern economic landscape, the visionaries who saw opportunities where others saw challenges, and the relentless pioneers who turned ideas into global empires. Their stories are not just tales of financial success but also of innovation, resilience, and the power of perseverance. This book is a tribute to those very titans — individuals whose names are synonymous with the industries they helped shape.

The purpose of Titans of Trade and Power is to delve into the lives of 10 Business Giants whose influence continues to ripple through the world today. From the creation of the first mass-produced automobile to the development of revolutionary tech products that have redefined our lives, these figures have built legacies that transcend their time. Their companies have not only transformed markets but have altered the very fabric of our society. They have shaped how we work, how we communicate, and how we live.

But this book is not merely about recounting the triumphs of these business giants. It is about understanding the foundational values that drove them — the unwavering vision that guided them through adversity, the risks they took when conventional wisdom said otherwise, and the lessons we can learn from their successes and failures.

As we journey through each chapter, we will explore the humble beginnings of these founders, the pivotal moments that propelled them to greatness, and their legacies that continue to shape the world. From the industrial revolution to the digital age, each of these titans carved out a space for themselves in history and, in doing so, set the stage for the modern world.

In their stories, we will uncover themes of innovation, ambition, and resilience. We will learn about the challenges they faced, the mistakes they made, and the lessons they imparted. Most importantly, we will see how these visionaries were able to take risks, embrace change, and build something that transcended their own lifetimes.

As we reflect on their journeys, it's important to recognize that their stories are not just for aspiring entrepreneurs or business professionals. They are for anyone who seeks to understand how determination, vision, and hard work can transform the world. Whether you are a student just beginning to explore the world of business, a seasoned professional looking for inspiration, or simply a curious reader interested in the great figures of history, this book offers something for everyone.

In writing this, I hope to offer a fresh perspective on the lives of these exceptional individuals and to inspire readers to pursue their own dreams, no matter how daunting they may seem. Just as these titans built empires from the ground up, so too can anyone achieve greatness with the right mindset, dedication, and vision.

This book is not merely a recounting of historical events; it is a collection of stories that speak to the potential within each of us to change the world. So, as you turn the pages, I invite you to reflect on the values and principles that these extraordinary individuals embodied and think about how you, too, can leave your mark on the world.

Acknowledgment For Editor Khalid Iqbal

It is with immense gratitude and heartfelt appreciation that we acknowledge the remarkable contributions of our esteemed editor, Khalid Iqbal, whose unwavering dedication, insightful guidance, and exceptional expertise have been integral to the creation of this book. From its inception to its final form, Khalid Iqbal has been a cornerstone of this project, providing not only meticulous editorial precision but also invaluable creative insights that have enriched every chapter.

Your ability to weave together historical accuracy, engaging storytelling, and a cohesive narrative has elevated this work to a level we had only dreamed of achieving. With your sharp eye for detail and unparalleled command of language, you have ensured that the stories of history's greatest business leaders are presented in a manner that is both compelling and accessible to readers.

Beyond the technical aspects of editing, your encouragement and support have been a beacon of light throughout this journey. Whether it was offering thoughtful suggestions, solving narrative challenges, or refining the tone to resonate with a wide audience, your efforts have been indispensable. Your passion for excellence and your belief in this project have motivated us to push boundaries and strive for the highest standards.

This book is as much a testament to your dedication as it is to the vision and legacy of the leaders it chronicles. We are deeply grateful for your partnership in bringing this work to life and for your role in ensuring that their stories will inspire readers for generations to come.

Thank you, Mohammad Khalid Iqbal , for your tireless efforts, creative brilliance, and unwavering commitment. This book would not have been possible without you.

Part I: The Pioneers of Industry

Part I: The Pioneers of Industry serves as both an homage to and a deep exploration of the transformative figures whose ingenuity and determination carved the path for modern entrepreneurship and industry. This section of the autobiography immerses readers in the lives and legacies of the great industrialists and business visionaries who defined their eras with daring innovation and unyielding ambition. These pioneers—names synonymous with progress and power—did more than build enterprises; they sparked revolutions that forever altered the landscape of commerce, manufacturing, and technology.

The author meticulously recounts the stories of these trailblazers, delving into the challenges they faced, the calculated risks they took, and the sheer tenacity they embodied to overcome the uncertainties of their time. From the electrifying breakthroughs of Thomas Edison and the transformational production methods of Henry Ford to the visionary financial strategies of J.P. Morgan and the industrial empires of Andrew Carnegie and John D. Rockefeller, each chapter paints a vivid picture of how these giants turned dreams into tangible legacies.

What sets this part apart is its interwoven narrative, blending historical accounts with the author's personal reflections and lessons learned. The author draws on the parallels between these pioneering journeys and his own path in business, illustrating how their timeless strategies and philosophies informed his decisions and helped him navigate the complex world of modern industry. Readers will discover how the roots of innovation, strategic alliances, and relentless pursuit of efficiency—hallmarks of the early industrial age—continue to echo in contemporary business practices.

The chapters are rich with anecdotes that capture pivotal moments: the late nights spent experimenting with prototypes, the fierce rivalries that fueled competition and progress, and the turning points when bold bets paid off against all odds. This narrative isn't just a recounting of history; it's an examination of what it truly means to be a pioneer—how these individuals overcame immense odds, adapted to challenges, and persevered when others doubted their visions.

By exploring the legacies of these titans of industry, the author sets the foundation for understanding the core principles that guide successful entrepreneurship today. Readers will gain insight into how these stories of ambition and innovation shaped not only the author's approach to building his own empire but also how they continue to influence global economic strategies and inspire future generations of business leaders. Part I establishes that to truly comprehend the art and science of industry, one must first appreciate the courage and foresight of the pioneers who dared to push the boundaries of possibility.

CHAPTER ONE

JAMSETJI NUSSERWANJI TATA – TATA GROUP'S

(History of Jamsetji Nusserwanji Tata and Tata Group's)

The Tata Group's history is deeply intertwined with the life and vision of its founder, Jamsetji Nusserwanji Tata, who is often regarded as the "Father of Indian Industry." Born on March 3, 1839, in the town of Navsari, Gujarat, into a Parsi Zoroastrian family, Jamsetji's upbringing laid the foundation for what would become one of the most influential business empires in the world.

Early Life and Education

Jamsetji's father, Nusserwanji Tata, was a small-scale businessman and the first member of the Tata family to embark on entrepreneurial ventures. Growing up, Jamsetji witnessed his father's persistence and ingenuity, which would later inspire his own approach to business. The young Jamsetji was educated in Navsari before moving to Bombay (now Mumbai), where he attended Elphinstone College, a premier educational institution at the time. Graduating in 1858, Jamsetji's formative years were marked by exposure to the social and economic changes occurring under British colonial rule.

His college years coincided with significant political upheaval—the 1857 Rebellion, which led to the dissolution of the East India Company and the establishment of direct British rule over India. This period of change instilled in Jamsetji a strong desire to see India flourish independently, sparking ideas that would later shape his industrial ventures.

Initial Forays into Business

After completing his education, Jamsetji joined his father's trading firm, where he learned the intricacies of commerce and enterprise. Early in his career, he traveled extensively, gaining insights into global trade networks and business practices. It was during these travels that Jamsetji developed an appreciation for the technological advancements that were revolutionizing industries in Europe and America. He envisioned India embracing similar progress to become a powerful industrial nation.

One of the key turning points in Jamsetji's early career came during the American Civil War (1861-1865). The conflict disrupted the global cotton supply, leading to a surge in demand for Indian cotton exports. Jamsetji seized this opportunity, establishing his own trading firm to supply raw cotton to British textile mills. This strategic move provided him with the financial capital needed to pursue more ambitious projects.

The Founding of Empress Mills

In 1874, Jamsetji's entrepreneurial vision culminated in the creation of the Empress Mills in Nagpur. Unlike most mills of the era that were marked by poor working conditions and obsolete technology, Empress Mills was groundbreaking in its approach. Jamsetji invested in modern machinery and infrastructure that improved efficiency and productivity. He also introduced progressive labor policies, offering workers benefits such as accident insurance, pension plans, and decent working conditions—a rarity in that era.

Jamsetji's commitment to the well-being of his employees was rooted in his belief that a business's success was intertwined with the welfare of its workforce. His ideas on employee welfare were far ahead of their time and set the Tata Group apart as an enterprise that valued human capital as much as financial capital. These principles would become the bedrock of the Tata Group's legacy of corporate social responsibility.

The Vision for a New India

Empress Mills established Jamsetji as a formidable industrialist, but his ambitions extended far beyond the confines of textile manufacturing. He envisioned a series of transformative projects that would lay the groundwork for India's industrial self-sufficiency. Three of his most notable visions included:

The Tata Iron and Steel Company (TISCO): Jamsetji's dream of setting up a steel plant was driven by his belief that India needed its own sources of steel to become a global power. Though he did not live to see it completed, his vision came to fruition under his successors when TISCO (now Tata Steel) was established in Jamshedpur in 1907, becoming Asia's first integrated steel company.

Indian Institute of Science (IISc): Jamsetji was deeply committed to the advancement of education and research. He pledged substantial funds to create an institution that would promote scientific research and technological development in India. The IISc, founded in Bangalore (now Bengaluru), stands as a testament to his commitment to education and remains one of India's premier research institutions.

Hydroelectric Power: Jamsetji also sought to harness the power of nature to supply clean, renewable energy to support industrial growth. His plans for hydroelectric projects laid the foundation for what would later become the Tata Power Company, playing a crucial role in electrifying Mumbai and fostering industrial expansion.

A Legacy Beyond Business

Jamsetji Tata passed away in 1904, but his legacy endured through the continuation of his ambitious projects. His successors carried forward his vision, expanding the Tata Group into sectors including steel, energy, hospitality, and chemicals, among others. The Tata Group's core values of integrity, excellence, and social responsibility trace back to Jamsetji's belief in ethical business practices and nation-building.

Today, the Tata Group is a global conglomerate, respected not only for its business acumen but also for its commitment to social welfare and community development—values that were instilled by its visionary founder, Jamsetji Nusserwanji Tata. His pioneering spirit and dedication to creating an equitable and prosperous society laid the foundation for what would become one of the most enduring and impactful business legacies in the world.

There is one kind of charity common enough among us... It is that patchwork philanthropy which clothes the ragged, feeds the

poor, and heals the sick- Jamsetji Nusserwanji Tata.

(Rise of Jamsetji Nusserwanji Tata and Tata Group's)

The story of the Tata Group's ascent from a modest trading firm to a global conglomerate is marked by strategic vision, innovation, and a commitment to both economic progress and social betterment. Founded by Jamsetji Tata in 1868, the company initially focused on trading and textile manufacturing, but it was Jamsetji's far-reaching aspirations that would lay the groundwork for an industrial empire that would transform India and earn worldwide recognition. This narrative explores how Tata Group evolved into a multi-industry leader, the pioneering steps it took to achieve this growth, and the revolutions it brought to various sectors, all while expanding its footprint beyond national borders.

Strategic Vision and Early Foundations

Jamsetji Tata's entrepreneurial journey began with the establishment of a trading company in Bombay (now Mumbai), where he swiftly moved into cotton manufacturing with the founding of Empress Mills in 1874. While these early ventures were successful, it was Jamsetji's forward-thinking vision that truly set the stage for Tata's future. He understood that India's progress depended on the industrial and infrastructural advancements seen in Western countries.

During his travels to England, the United States, and other industrialized nations, Jamsetji studied innovations in engineering, metallurgy, and factory management. He envisioned a future where India would not merely supply raw materials but would also process and manufacture goods, adding value and fostering economic self-reliance. His early blueprint for growth included three major pillars: a world-class hotel, an iron and steel company, and a hydroelectric power plant—each of which would contribute to India's economic and social upliftment.

Establishing Tata Steel: A Milestone in Industrial Progress

One of the most significant milestones in Tata's history was the founding of Tata Iron and Steel Company (TISCO) in 1907, an achievement that marked the beginning of India's industrial revolution. While Jamsetji did not live to see this dream realized, his son, Sir Dorabji Tata, brought it to fruition. TISCO, established in Jamshedpur, became a cornerstone of industrial growth in India. Prior to its establishment, India relied heavily on imported steel, limiting its ability to build essential infrastructure and hindering industrial expansion.

TISCO's emergence revolutionized India's economic landscape. It supplied steel for major construction projects and contributed to the development of railways, bridges, and public infrastructure. Importantly, Tata Steel's emphasis on quality and efficiency soon gained international attention, positioning it as a competitive player in the global market. Beyond its economic impact, the company pioneered employee welfare practices rarely seen at the time, such as providing worker housing, healthcare, and education, which laid the groundwork for future labor policies.

Diversification and Entry Into New Sectors

As Tata Steel solidified its position, the Tata Group began diversifying its operations to mitigate risk and capitalize on emerging opportunities. The group entered the energy sector with the establishment of Tata Power in 1911. This move was inspired by Jamsetji's vision of harnessing hydroelectric power to generate clean, renewable energy. Tata Power's creation was groundbreaking for India, which was still largely dependent on coal and other traditional energy sources. The company's successful implementation of hydroelectric projects demonstrated that India could innovate and adopt sustainable practices long before such efforts became globally recognized priorities.

The diversification continued with the founding of Tata Chemicals in the 1930s. This venture was pivotal as it bolstered the Indian chemical industry, allowing the country to reduce its dependence on imports for essential industrial chemicals. Tata Chemicals' foray into products that supported agriculture and various industries further reinforced Tata's reputation for fostering national self-sufficiency.

World War II and Post-War Expansion

The Tata Group's operations were tested during World War II, as the demand for steel and other materials skyrocketed. TISCO played a critical role in supplying steel for defense and construction, showcasing its capacity to meet high-demand conditions and establishing its reputation as a reliable industrial partner.

After the war, under the leadership of J.R.D. Tata, the group embarked on an ambitious expansion phase that would redefine its identity. J.R.D., who became chairman in 1938, was instrumental in modernizing the group's management practices and pursuing growth in new industries. He emphasized technological innovation, quality, and strategic investments that would propel Tata Group beyond India's borders.

The Rise of Tata Motors and Engineering Innovations

One of the most notable expansions under J.R.D.'s tenure was Tata Motors (originally TELCO), established in 1945 to manufacture locomotives and engineering products. As India gained independence in 1947, the need for robust domestic industries became more urgent, and Tata Motors evolved to meet this demand. Initially focused on commercial vehicles such as trucks and buses, the company quickly became an essential player in India's transportation sector.

By the 1990s, Tata Motors diversified into passenger vehicles, leveraging its experience and technological capabilities. The launch of the Tata Indica in 1998 was a game-changer, marking the first passenger car designed, developed, and manufactured entirely in India. This achievement underscored Tata's engineering capabilities and commitment to producing high-quality, locally made products that could compete on the global stage.

Global Expansion and High-Profile Acquisitions

The 21st century heralded a new era for Tata Group marked by strategic international acquisitions and partnerships. This phase began in earnest with Tata Tea's acquisition of Tetley in 2000, making Tata Tea the second-largest tea company in the world. The move was strategic, as it positioned Tata within global consumer markets and provided an avenue for leveraging international supply chains and expertise.

Perhaps the most notable expansion came in 2008 with Tata Motors' acquisition of Jaguar and Land Rover (JLR) from Ford. This acquisition was bold and risky, but it proved transformative. Despite early challenges, including a global recession, Tata Motors successfully revitalized the luxury brands, infusing them with innovation and aligning them with new market trends. This move demonstrated Tata's ambition to step beyond Indian borders and establish itself as a global automotive leader.

Pioneering Technology with Tata Consultancy Services (TCS)

The digital era brought new opportunities, and Tata Group's foresight led to the creation of Tata Consultancy Services (TCS) in 1968. Initially set up as a division within Tata Sons, TCS evolved into a leading provider of IT services, business solutions, and outsourcing. By anticipating the rise of the digital economy and investing in technological capabilities, TCS positioned itself as a global leader in IT services by the 2000s.

TCS's expansion into international markets and its commitment to quality and innovation solidified its standing as one of the most valuable subsidiaries within the group. Today, TCS is a key contributor to Tata's global revenue and continues to drive digital transformation across industries.

The Tata Philosophy: Business With a Purpose

A distinguishing feature of Tata Group's rise has been its adherence to a business philosophy that values profit alongside societal impact. This principle was deeply embedded in Jamsetji Tata's original vision and carried forward by subsequent leaders. The Tata philanthropic trusts, established by Sir Dorabji Tata and later expanded, have funded initiatives in healthcare, education, and scientific research, reflecting a belief that business success should translate into community upliftment.

During J.R.D. Tata's leadership, the group formalized its approach to corporate responsibility and governance. Policies were implemented that emphasized fair labor practices, environmental sustainability, and community development. Under Ratan Tata, who took over as chairman in 1991, this ethos was further reinforced. Ratan Tata's tenure saw the group expanding its focus on affordability and accessibility, highlighted by the launch of the Tata Nano in 2009—the world's most affordable car designed to provide personal transportation to millions of Indian families.

Challenges and Triumphs

Despite its successes, the Tata Group has faced numerous challenges. Economic downturns, global competition, and internal restructuring have tested the group's resilience. The 2008 financial crisis was particularly challenging for Tata Motors and its JLR acquisition. Yet, through strategic leadership, cost management, and a focus on innovation, Tata Motors turned JLR into a profitable venture within a few years.

The group's ability to adapt and reinvent itself has been crucial. For instance, Tata Steel's acquisition of Corus in 2007 was a strategic move to enhance its global steel production capabilities. While the integration posed initial difficulties, it ultimately strengthened Tata Steel's position in the global market.

Continued Growth

Today, Tata Group stands as a symbol of India's industrial prowess and global ambitions, with operations in more than 100 countries and over 100 subsidiaries. Its legacy, rooted in the visionary ideas of Jamsetji Tata, continues through new ventures in fields such as renewable energy, e-commerce, and advanced materials. The group's enduring focus on sustainability, innovation, and community impact ensures that it remains relevant in an ever-changing global landscape.

The rise of Tata Group is not just a story of business success; it is a narrative of visionaries who believed in creating lasting value for society. From its pioneering steel plants and hydroelectric projects to its foray into technology and global markets, Tata's journey reflects a blend of ambition, resilience, and an unwavering commitment to ethical practices and social responsibility.

(Currrent Status of Tata Group's)

The Tata Group, a global giant with a legacy spanning over 150 years, stands as one of the most influential conglomerates in the world. This document provides an in-depth look into the current state of the Tata Group, its leadership, family involvement, and its unparalleled philanthropic contributions. Through its strategic leadership and the enduring legacy of its founders, the Tata Group continues to thrive and adapt, balancing profitability with social responsibility.

Current Leadership and Management Structure

The Tata Group is presently chaired by Natarajan Chandrasekaran, who took over as Executive Chairman in 2017. His appointment followed a turbulent period marked by internal disputes and the removal of Cyrus Mistry as chairman. Chandrasekaran's leadership, often characterized by innovation and sustainability, has significantly transformed the group's operations, leading it toward modernizing traditional businesses while expanding into new sectors such as renewable energy and e-commerce.

Before becoming chairman, Chandrasekaran had an illustrious career within Tata Consultancy Services (TCS), where he played a key role in its transformation into one of the world's largest and most profitable IT services firms. Under his guidance, TCS not only solidified its position in the global market but also aligned itself with emerging technologies such as cloud computing and artificial intelligence. Chandrasekaran's strategic foresight has further extended to other businesses in the group, reinforcing their competitive positions in global markets.

The leadership challenges during the transition period, particularly following Mistry's ousting, highlighted the influence of Tata Trusts, which hold the majority stake in Tata Sons, the holding company of the Tata Group. This ensured that the group's foundational values remained intact despite the corporate turbulence.

The Legacy of Ratan Tata and His Continuing Influence

Ratan Tata, whose tenure as chairman from 1991 to 2012 is considered one of the most transformative periods for the group, continues to be a guiding influence within Tata Group. Although officially retired, Tata's leadership legacy remains an intrinsic part of the conglomerate's identity. Under his stewardship, Tata Group made significant global acquisitions, such as Tetley (2000), Corus Group (2007), and Jaguar Land Rover (2008), which elevated its global presence and diversified its portfolio.

Tata's most notable initiative during his tenure was the development of the Tata Nano, a car designed to make personal transportation affordable to the masses, reflecting his commitment to social good. While the Nano project faced commercial challenges, it epitomized Tata's vision of inclusivity, demonstrating the group's willingness to take bold risks in pursuit of social welfare.

Ratan Tata also solidified the Tata Group's reputation for ethical business practices, aligning business success with broader societal impact. His tenure emphasized values such as integrity, transparency, and respect for people, all of which remain central to the group's operations today.

The Tata Family's Role and Their Connection to the Business

While the Tata Group operates as a complex and globally diversified conglomerate, the Tata family, particularly through Tata Trusts, maintains a significant influence on its strategic direction. The family's involvement in governance is primarily channeled through the philanthropic trusts that own around 66% of Tata Sons, the parent company of the Tata Group.

The Sir Dorabji Tata Trust and the Sir Ratan Tata Trust are two key entities through which the Tata family exercises its influence. These trusts play a crucial role in the group's charitable activities, ensuring that profits are directed toward societal causes, ranging from education and healthcare to disaster relief and rural development. Ratan Tata himself remains active in the group's philanthropic efforts, continuing to embody the Tata family's commitment to business practices that prioritize social welfare over individual wealth accumulation.

Philanthropic Contributions and Charitable Work

The Tata Group's dedication to philanthropy is one of its defining characteristics. This commitment traces back to Jamsetji Tata, the founder of the Tata Group, who believed that businesses should contribute to the betterment of society. The philanthropic efforts of the Tata family and Tata Trusts have continued to flourish, with the group playing a leading role in healthcare, education, disaster relief, and sustainable development.

Healthcare and Education Initiatives

Tata Trusts has made substantial contributions to healthcare, with institutions like Tata Memorial Hospital serving as one of the world's leading cancer treatment and research centers. The Indian Institute of Science (IISc), which was established through Jamsetji Tata's endowment, remains a key institution for scientific research and education in India.

Ratan Tata continued this legacy by fostering education initiatives, including the Tata Education and Development Trust, which launched scholarships to empower underprivileged students. The trust's $28 million endowment to Cornell

University for supporting Indian students highlights the Tata Group's global philanthropic impact.

Disaster Relief and Community Development

The Tata Group has also been a leader in disaster relief and community support. From aiding the victims of the 2004 Indian Ocean tsunami to supporting communities during the COVID-19 pandemic, the group has consistently been at the forefront of humanitarian efforts. During the COVID-19 crisis, Tata Trusts and Tata Sons pledged over $200 million in relief efforts, providing medical supplies, vaccine research funding, and frontline worker support.

Environmental Sustainability and Renewable Energy

The group's commitment to sustainability is seen in its initiatives aimed at reducing environmental impact. Tata Power's efforts in providing solar-powered microgrids to rural areas, Tata Steel's commitment to reducing carbon emissions, and Tata Motors' push toward electric vehicles are prime examples of the group's approach to combining business success with environmental responsibility.

The Role of Tata Consultancy Services (TCS)

TCS remains the crown jewel of the Tata Group, contributing a significant portion of the conglomerate's revenue. As a leader in IT services, TCS has consistently adapted to technological advancements, ensuring that both the group and its clients remain competitive in an increasingly digital world. In addition to its financial success, TCS has contributed to educational and skill development programs, promoting digital literacy and vocational training across India.

Ratan Tata: A Visionary Leader

Ratan Tata, who served as the chairman of Tata Group from 1991 to 2012, is widely regarded as one of the most influential corporate figures globally. His leadership was marked by groundbreaking acquisitions such as Tetley, Corus, and Jaguar Land Rover, which helped propel the Tata Group into the global spotlight. Under Ratan Tata's stewardship, the company's focus expanded beyond profit to emphasize social contributions and ethical governance.

One of the hallmarks of his tenure was the launch of the Tata Nano, an ambitious project aimed at providing affordable cars to the masses. Despite challenges in the market, the Nano represented Tata's vision of addressing societal issues through innovation. Even after retiring, Ratan Tata's philanthropic efforts remain a central aspect of his legacy, with significant contributions to fields such as education and healthcare through Tata Trusts.

Ratan Tata's commitment to philanthropy extended beyond his corporate role. Notably, he donated a substantial portion of his personal wealth to various causes and spearheaded initiatives such as the Tata Memorial Hospital and the Indian Institute of Science, ensuring that these institutions would provide lasting benefits to society.

I don't believe in taking right decisions. I take decisions and then make them right.-Rata Tata

Leadership Succession and Future Outlook

While Natarajan Chandrasekaran continues to steer the Tata Group as chairman, the conglomerate is also focusing on grooming the next generation of leaders. This focus on leadership succession ensures that the group remains responsive to global challenges, particularly in the realms of technology and sustainability.

The group's ongoing ventures into electric mobility, artificial intelligence, and digital solutions suggest a forward-looking strategy aimed at not only sustaining but expanding its market presence. Tata Motors' investments in electric vehicle technology and the group's push for renewable energy and digital innovation align with the broader trends of the 21st century, signaling Tata's commitment to adapting and thriving in a rapidly changing global economy.

The Impact of Family and Legacy

The Tata family's commitment to philanthropy remains one of the most profound aspects of the Tata Group's identity. Unlike many other business families, the Tata family has consistently prioritized collective welfare over personal wealth, shaping a corporate culture that places social impact at the heart of its mission. This legacy, founded by Jamsetji Tata, continues to guide the group's approach to business, ensuring that the company's growth is always accompanied by contributions to society. This philosophy not only defines the group's corporate ethos but also sets a high standard for corporate responsibility worldwide.

The Stock Growth and Financial Health

The financial health of the Tata Group is primarily driven by Tata Consultancy Services (TCS), the group's flagship IT services company. TCS consistently ranks as one of the top companies in India by market capitalization, contributing significantly to the group's stock growth and global recognition.

In addition to TCS, the Tata Motors segment, especially its investment in electric vehicles, aligns the group with future sustainability trends. The Tata Group has been proactive in diversifying its business portfolio, which now includes renewable energy and AI-based solutions, signaling a commitment to long-term growth in these innovative sectors.

Philanthropy: The Tata Group's Defining Trait

A unique feature of the Tata Group is its unwavering commitment to philanthropy, which is deeply embedded in its corporate DNA. Tata Trusts, controlling much of Tata Sons, directs significant funding toward societal initiatives, ranging from healthcare to education and disaster relief. Over the years, the Tata Group has funded the Tata Memorial Cancer Hospital, supported IISc for cutting-edge research, and played a crucial role in disaster relief efforts, including contributions during the 2004 tsunami and COVID-19 pandemic.

Ratan Tata's philanthropic influence remains strong, evidenced by his personal donations to causes such as Cornell University, where he made a generous $28 million endowment to support underprivileged students, particularly from India.

CHAPTER TWO

JOHN D. ROCKEFELLER – STANDARD OIL

(History of John D. Rockefeller and Standard Oil Company)

Introduction

John D. Rockefeller, an American industrialist and philanthropist, is widely regarded as one of the wealthiest individuals in modern history. As the co-founder and head of Standard Oil, he played a pivotal role in shaping the American oil industry and establishing practices that would go on to define modern business practices worldwide. Despite his significant contributions to industrial growth, his methods and the resulting monopolistic control of the oil industry have remained contentious, with critics accusing him of using unethical practices to dominate and stifle competition.

Through Standard Oil, Rockefeller revolutionized the oil industry, introducing new technologies, refining processes, and marketing strategies. His story is a complex one—marked by immense wealth, transformative business tactics, and a lasting influence that continues to shape modern industry. This narrative covers the history of Rockefeller and his company, tracing their origins, their rise to dominance, and their eventual downfall, as well as the lasting legacy of Standard Oil in the world of business.

Early Life of John D. Rockefeller

John D. Rockefeller was born on July 8, 1839, in Richford, New York, to William and Eliza Rockefeller. His father, a traveling salesman, was known for his shady business dealings and was often described as a "doctor of dubious character" who sold patent medicines. However, his mother was a devout Baptist, and she instilled in Rockefeller strong values of discipline, thrift, and religious faith, all of which would influence his business practices later in life.

Rockefeller's early education was modest, but he displayed an aptitude for numbers from a young age. He attended public schools and later went to a business school in Cleveland. His first job was as a bookkeeper at the age of 16, earning $3.75 a week, a sum he carefully saved. This early experience in finance and accounting provided the foundation for his future career as a business magnate. Rockefeller's disciplined approach to money and his meticulous nature were key factors that would later contribute to his success in the competitive world of oil.

The Formation of Standard Oil

Rockefeller's entry into the oil business began in 1859, when Edwin L. Drake successfully drilled the first oil well in Titusville, Pennsylvania, which marked the beginning of the modern oil industry. At the time, oil was primarily used for lighting, but it had limited industrial applications. However, the discovery of petroleum would quickly revolutionize the energy industry.

In 1863, Rockefeller, along with his partners, invested in a small oil refinery in Cleveland, Ohio. He was able to capitalize on the increasing demand for refined oil, largely driven by the growing market for kerosene lamps. Recognizing the immense potential of oil, Rockefeller worked tirelessly to expand his refining operations. Within a few years, his firm, Rockefeller & Andrews, would become one of the largest refiners in Cleveland.

In 1870, Rockefeller co-founded Standard Oil of Ohio (SOHIO), the company that would later become synonymous with his name. The creation of Standard Oil marked a pivotal moment in the history of American business. Rockefeller had a clear vision for how he wanted to control the industry—by consolidating refining and distribution, gaining control over transportation (via pipelines and railroads), and reducing costs through economies of scale. Through a combination of business acumen, ruthlessness, and a willingness to innovate, Rockefeller began to dominate the oil industry.

First Pipeline of Standard Oil's

The Growth of Standard Oil

Rockefeller's approach to business was unorthodox for its time. He employed a strategy known as vertical integration, where a company controls every aspect of production, from raw materials to distribution. By acquiring or controlling the entire supply chain—such as oil wells, pipelines, refineries, and retail outlets—Rockefeller was able to eliminate inefficiencies and reduce costs. This gave Standard Oil a significant competitive edge, enabling the company to offer lower prices and generate more profits.

In addition to vertical integration, Rockefeller utilized horizontal integration to expand Standard Oil's dominance. He achieved this by buying out competitors and creating a network of affiliated companies, which effectively created a monopoly. By the late 1870s, Standard Oil controlled nearly 90% of the oil refining in the United States. This level of consolidation allowed Rockefeller to dictate prices and quality, often at the expense of smaller competitors.

Rockefeller's tactics included offering rebates to railroads for shipping Standard Oil's oil, which meant that smaller companies, who didn't have the same leverage, were forced to pay higher rates. He would also undercut competitors by selling oil at a loss in certain markets, driving them out of business. Once they were eliminated, Rockefeller would raise prices, often to levels that were much higher than before.

The company's aggressive tactics sparked intense criticism. Some saw Rockefeller as a ruthless monopolist who destroyed competition, while others viewed him as a brilliant entrepreneur who simply capitalized on an industry in need of order and efficiency. Despite the controversies, there was no denying that Rockefeller had transformed the oil industry and created one of the largest and most powerful companies in the world.

The Standard Oil Trust and Its Monopoly

In 1882, to consolidate his holdings and gain more control over his various interests, Rockefeller and his associates created the Standard Oil Trust. The trust was a legal structure that allowed Standard Oil to operate under a unified management system, even though it was technically a collection of separate companies. This innovative organizational structure gave Rockefeller unprecedented control over the oil industry.

Under the trust, Rockefeller was able to further consolidate power. The trust included both vertically and horizontally integrated companies, making it nearly impossible for competitors to challenge Standard Oil. Rockefeller's monopoly extended across almost every part of the oil industry, from drilling to distribution.

While Standard Oil's success was undeniable, the company faced increasing scrutiny from the public and the government. As the trust expanded, so did concerns about its size and power. Critics argued that Standard Oil was an example of monopolistic behavior that stifled competition, manipulated prices, and exploited workers.

Legal Challenges and the Breakup of Standard Oil

In the early 20th century, public opinion shifted dramatically against the monopolistic practices of big corporations like Standard Oil. The Progressive Era, a period of social and political reform, saw growing calls for antitrust laws that would limit the power of monopolies and promote fair competition. The Sherman Antitrust Act of 1890 was a key piece of legislation in this movement, aimed at curbing the power of monopolies and trusts.

In 1906, the federal government took action against Standard Oil, accusing it of violating antitrust laws. The case eventually made its way to the U.S. Supreme Court, which ruled in 1911 that Standard Oil must be broken up into 34 smaller companies. The court's decision was based on the claim that Standard Oil had engaged in anti-competitive practices and violated the Sherman Antitrust Act.

The breakup of Standard Oil marked the end of Rockefeller's domination of the oil industry. However, the legacy of Standard Oil continued, as many of the resulting companies would go on to become major players in the global oil market. Companies like ExxonMobil, Chevron, and Mobil, which are still household names today, trace their origins to the breakup of Standard Oil.

Although Rockefeller's company was dismantled, he remained a wealthy and influential figure. The breakup allowed him to continue making money from his various holdings, even as Standard Oil was dissolved. In fact, Rockefeller's wealth continued to grow even after the breakup, making him one of the wealthiest men in the world at the time.

Philanthropy and Legacy

After retiring from active business in 1897, John D. Rockefeller turned his focus toward philanthropy. Over the course of his life, he donated billions of dollars to various causes, including education, public health, scientific research, and religious organizations. One of his most significant philanthropic endeavors was the creation of the Rockefeller Foundation in 1913, which aimed to promote the well-being of humanity by supporting research and initiatives in fields such as public health, education, and the arts.

Rockefeller's charitable work helped to reshape the landscape of American philanthropy. His contributions were instrumental in the establishment of several prestigious institutions, including the University of Chicago and the Rockefeller Institute for Medical Research (now Rockefeller University). He also funded the construction of public libraries, health clinics, and educational institutions across the United States.

Despite the controversies surrounding his business practices, Rockefeller's philanthropic legacy remains one of the most significant in American history. His approach to giving was systematic and far-reaching, and his donations continue to benefit many institutions and causes today.

The Legacy of Standard Oil

The legacy of Standard Oil is complex. On one hand, the company's aggressive business practices and monopoly-building tactics are seen as an example of the darker side of capitalism. On the other hand, Standard Oil's innovations in refining, distribution, and marketing revolutionized the oil industry and set the stage for modern corporate practices. The company's legacy also highlights the tension between business efficiency and social responsibility, a theme that continues to be relevant in today's corporate world.

While the breakup of Standard Oil was seen as a victory for antitrust advocates, it also gave rise to some of the largest and most powerful oil companies in the world. Many of the companies that resulted from the breakup, such as ExxonMobil, Chevron, and ConocoPhillips, continue to play a dominant role in the global oil industry.

In many ways, the story of Standard Oil is the story of the rise of modern capitalism—marked by innovation, competition, and the drive for dominance. However, it is also a story of the challenges that come with unchecked corporate power and the need for regulation and oversight to ensure that companies serve the public interest.

Rockefeller's Strategic Business Practices and Innovation

John D. Rockefeller was a pioneer in many aspects of business strategy. He was highly focused on maximizing efficiency, minimizing costs, and constantly innovating in every part of his operation. This drove Standard Oil's dominance and success throughout the late 19th and early 20th centuries. In addition to vertical and horizontal integration, Rockefeller's management style was one of careful control, and he sought to streamline every process from drilling to distribution.

One of his key innovations was the introduction of pipelines to transport oil, which radically changed how the oil industry operated. At the time, most oil was transported via railroads, but Rockefeller recognized that pipelines could offer a cheaper and more efficient alternative. In 1879, Standard Oil built its first pipeline, allowing it to bypass the railroads, cut transportation costs, and gain an edge over competitors. This move not only reduced Standard Oil's reliance on third-party transport companies but also helped standardize the flow of oil across large distances, which had never been done before in the industry.

Another key innovation by Rockefeller was the development of the refining process itself. Standard Oil invested heavily in new refining techniques, improving the quality of oil products and increasing output. The company's refineries were able to process oil more efficiently, producing kerosene and other byproducts at a much higher rate than competitors. This allowed Rockefeller to offer his products at lower prices, which forced his competitors to either match those prices or go out of business.

Additionally, Rockefeller's interest in innovation extended to the creation of new markets for oil-based products. While kerosene was the primary product derived from crude oil, Rockefeller was quick to recognize the emerging potential of gasoline, a byproduct of the refining process. As the automobile industry began to grow in the early 20th century, Rockefeller's foresight allowed him to capitalize on the growing demand for gasoline, securing a dominant position in what would later become one of the most lucrative segments of the oil business.

Standard Oil's technological and process innovations were not limited to oil refining. Rockefeller's firm was a key player in the development of the infrastructure required to move, store, and sell oil products. He worked with the railroads and shipping companies to ensure that Standard Oil's products were distributed efficiently and quickly across the country. This kind of innovation and control over the logistics of the oil business gave Standard Oil an immense advantage in the market, which no competitor could easily replicate.

Rockefeller's Philosophy of Business and Efficiency

John D. Rockefeller's view of business was shaped by his strong belief in efficiency and rational organization. He adhered to a strict philosophy of business that prioritized cost-cutting and eliminating waste. He believed that businesses should operate with military precision, and he demanded that his managers adhere to this philosophy. The result was a company that was highly centralized and organized, with careful oversight of every aspect of its operations.

Rockefeller was known for his commitment to continual improvement. He emphasized the importance of analyzing every part of the company's operations to find inefficiencies and eliminate them. Standard Oil's corporate structure was tightly controlled, with divisions responsible for each part of the oil business. This allowed for effective management and ensured that the company could operate at the highest level of efficiency.

He was also a firm believer in the concept of economies of scale—believing that the larger a company grew, the more cost-effective and efficient it would become. By increasing the size of Standard Oil's operations and consolidating market share, Rockefeller was able to further reduce costs and increase profitability. The company's size gave it tremendous leverage over suppliers, distributors, and even government entities, allowing it to set its own terms and dominate the market.

However, Rockefeller's focus on efficiency was not without its consequences. His methods were criticized for being overly aggressive, and his firm was often accused of undercutting competitors and manipulating prices. Critics argued that his pursuit of efficiency sometimes came at the expense of fair competition and consumer choice. Nonetheless, Rockefeller's philosophy of efficiency helped transform the oil industry and laid the groundwork for modern corporate management practices.

Rockefeller's Political and Economic Influence

In addition to his dominance over the oil industry, John D. Rockefeller wielded considerable political and economic power. His immense wealth allowed him to gain influence over politicians, and his business practices attracted the attention of lawmakers and regulators. Rockefeller used his wealth and influence to push for favorable policies and protect his company from government interference.

Rockefeller's political influence was not limited to bribery or underhanded dealings. He also used his position to advocate for policies that he believed would benefit the country. For instance, he supported the idea of government regulation of the oil industry, arguing that it would provide stability and prevent overproduction. His reasoning was that regulated production would keep prices stable and allow oil to be distributed more efficiently across the country. However, many saw his support for regulation as self-serving, believing that he wanted to ensure that his company would be the one to benefit from such policies.

Rockefeller's economic influence was also evident in his ability to shape the market. Through his control over transportation and refining, he had the power to set prices and control the supply of oil. This made it difficult for competitors to challenge Standard Oil, as they could not match Rockefeller's prices or compete with his superior distribution network. By controlling such a large portion of the oil industry, Rockefeller became one of the most influential figures in the U.S. economy, and his actions reverberated across the global markets.

The Public Backlash and the Rise of Antitrust Movements

While Rockefeller's business practices were initially hailed as a model of efficiency and success, as Standard Oil's power grew, so did the public backlash. As the company's monopoly expanded, it became more difficult for consumers and politicians to ignore the negative impact it was having on competition and the market. Smaller competitors were being driven out of business, and consumers were often left with limited choices for oil products.

The public's growing dissatisfaction with monopolistic practices came to a head in the late 19th and early 20th centuries. The Progressive Era, marked by growing support for social reforms, saw increasing calls for government intervention to curb the power of large corporations. Critics of Standard Oil, such as muckraking journalists like Ida Tarbell, helped expose the less savory aspects of Rockefeller's business empire. Tarbell's landmark investigative reporting in McClure's Magazine in the early 1900s was instrumental in shaping public opinion and bringing attention to the monopolistic practices employed by Standard Oil.

The government responded to these concerns with legal action. The Sherman Antitrust Act, passed in 1890, was the first significant federal legislation aimed at curbing monopolistic behavior. In 1911, the U.S. Supreme Court ruled that Standard Oil had violated the Sherman Antitrust Act, and the company was ordered to break up into 34 smaller, independent companies.

This decision marked the end of Standard Oil as a single entity, but its legacy lived on. The companies that resulted from the breakup, such as Exxon, Mobil, Chevron, and others, became major players in the oil industry. These companies, which had once been part of Rockefeller's empire, continued to dominate the market for decades to come.

The Philanthropic Legacy of John D. Rockefeller

After stepping down from the day-to-day operations of Standard Oil, Rockefeller dedicated himself to philanthropy. His later years were marked by a profound commitment to giving back to society, and he became one of the most prominent philanthropists of his time. Rockefeller's charitable contributions were vast and touched many areas of society, including education, health, and scientific research.

Rockefeller's philanthropic efforts included the creation of the Rockefeller Foundation in 1913, which focused on public health, education, and scientific research. He donated large sums of money to the University of Chicago, which he helped establish, and to medical institutions, including the Rockefeller Institute for Medical Research (now Rockefeller University). In total, it is estimated that Rockefeller gave away more than $500 million during his lifetime—an amount equivalent to several billion dollars today.

His philanthropic work is seen as one of the most significant contributions made by any business magnate. While some critics argue that his charitable donations were a way for him to restore his public image, others view his philanthropic legacy as a reflection of his deep belief in the responsibility of the wealthy to give back to society.

(Rise of Standard OIL and John D. Rockefeller)

The Rise of John D. Rockefeller and Standard Oil

Introduction: The Emergence of an Industrial Giant

The rise of John D. Rockefeller and the creation of Standard Oil is a story marked by ambition, innovation, and strategic brilliance, underpinned by a period of rapid industrialization in the United States. Born into humble beginnings, Rockefeller's ascent from a young bookkeeper to the wealthiest man in modern history was not just a result of his business acumen, but also of his groundbreaking strategies that transformed the oil industry and corporate America itself. Rockefeller's Standard Oil would not only dominate the oil industry, but also redefine the concept of business empires, setting the stage for the corporate monopolies and industrial giants of the 20th century.

The origins of Standard Oil are intricately tied to Rockefeller's belief in efficiency, control, and his obsession with eliminating competition. It is within this vision that the rise of Standard Oil was conceived, with Rockefeller positioning himself as not just a participant, but a master of the burgeoning oil industry. The early days of Standard Oil were marked by intense competition, technological advancements, and strategic maneuvers that would later lead to the formation of one of the most powerful and influential companies in the world.

Early Life and the Seeds of Ambition

John D. Rockefeller was born on July 8, 1839, in Richford, New York, to William Rockefeller and Eliza Davison. His father was a traveling salesman who often lived apart from the family, and his mother raised him with a strong sense of religious discipline and a commitment to hard work. Rockefeller's early life was modest, but he demonstrated a remarkable ability to understand and manage money from a young age. As a child, he often sold candies and was known for his careful attention to pricing and maximizing profit.

Rockefeller's formal education was brief, ending when he was 16 years old. Despite this, his work ethic and business acumen were apparent early on. In 1855, at the age of 16, Rockefeller secured a job as an assistant bookkeeper at Hewitt & Tuttle, a produce commission business in Cleveland. Here, he began learning the intricacies of business operations, finance, and accounting. It was at this job that he first encountered the concept of making profits by providing services that ensured reliability, stability, and efficiency.

In 1859, the discovery of oil in Pennsylvania by Edwin Drake ushered in an era of opportunity. It was during this period of rapid development in the oil industry that Rockefeller saw an opportunity to build an empire. While the oil industry was still in its infancy, with oil mostly used as a crude source for lighting lamps, Rockefeller quickly recognized the potential for enormous profits. By 1863, he decided to enter the oil business, investing in his first oil refinery in Cleveland with a partner, Maurice B. Clark.

The Formation of Standard Oil: Strategic Vision and Early Successes

Rockefeller's entry into the oil business was not accidental. At the time, the oil industry was fragmented, with many small, independent refineries competing for market share. The oil refining process was inefficient, and prices for oil were volatile. As Rockefeller began building his refinery business, he focused on improving the quality of his products while reducing production costs, which allowed him to offer kerosene at competitive prices. However, the real turning point in his career came when he devised a business strategy that would forever change the landscape of the oil industry: vertical integration.

Vertical integration is the practice of controlling all aspects of production, from raw material extraction to transportation, refinement, and distribution. Rockefeller quickly realized that to dominate the oil industry, he needed to control not only the refining process but also the sources of crude oil, transportation infrastructure, and the distribution of finished products. In doing so, he would be able to eliminate waste, reduce costs, and increase efficiency.

By 1865, Rockefeller had expanded his refinery operations, and through a series of calculated mergers, he began to consolidate the oil industry in Cleveland. In a remarkably short time, he had outpaced most of his competitors, acquiring smaller refineries and absorbing their operations into his own. Standard Oil, as it became known, was built through this aggressive, strategic process of horizontal integration. By the early 1870s, Rockefeller controlled the lion's share of oil refining in the United States, securing a monopoly in Ohio.

The Growth of Standard Oil and Rockefeller's Business Tactics

As Rockefeller's refining empire expanded, he continued to push for efficiencies that would further solidify his dominance. One of his most important moves was to secure favorable transportation contracts with railroads. The cost of shipping oil was a major expense for oil producers, and Rockefeller recognized that by securing discounted rates, he could outcompete other refineries. Through a combination of strategic partnerships and under-the-table deals with railroads, Rockefeller gained exclusive access to transportation networks, giving Standard Oil an advantage that no competitor could match.

Additionally, Rockefeller was not above using aggressive tactics to eliminate competition. One of his most notorious strategies was the practice of price undercutting. He would temporarily lower prices to a point where smaller competitors could no longer afford to operate and were forced to sell their refineries to Standard Oil. This tactic helped him expand his empire even further, leaving few competitors in his wake. Through these tactics, combined with his business acumen and commitment to efficiency, Standard Oil continued to dominate the oil industry.

The Formation of the Standard Oil Trust: A New Era of Corporate Power

By the late 1870s, Rockefeller's success in the oil industry was undeniable. Standard Oil had established itself as a monopolistic force in the refining sector, but Rockefeller's ambitions were not limited to refining alone. He began to extend his influence into other areas of the oil industry, including oil drilling, transportation, and marketing. His most significant move came in 1882, when he consolidated his interests into the Standard Oil Trust, a legal entity that allowed him to centralize control over a wide array of companies while maintaining a degree of independence for each individual refinery. This structure allowed Rockefeller and his partners to operate with even greater coordination and efficiency.

The trust mechanism essentially enabled Standard Oil to control a massive network of refineries, pipelines, and oil wells, while minimizing the need for direct ownership. The creation of the Standard Oil Trust gave Rockefeller more control over the oil industry than any single individual in the history of American business. The new corporate structure was immensely successful and cemented Rockefeller's place at the head of the oil industry. Standard Oil's efficiency was unmatched, and its profits soared as the company expanded both domestically and internationally.

Challenges and Expansion into New Markets

By the 1880s, Standard Oil had not only dominated the U.S. oil market, but it was also looking to expand its influence beyond American borders. Rockefeller sought international markets where oil production was still in its infancy, and his company began to develop an extensive network of operations overseas. This expansion helped Standard Oil to increase its market share and solidify its position as a global force in the oil industry.

However, Standard Oil's success was not without challenges. As the company continued to grow, it faced increasing public scrutiny. Critics accused Rockefeller of using unscrupulous tactics to eliminate competition and establish a monopoly, and some began to question whether such a concentration of power was healthy for the economy. In particular, there was growing resentment over Rockefeller's influence over prices, transportation, and the lack of competition in the oil market.

In the face of increasing opposition, Rockefeller was forced to defend his business practices. He maintained that his methods were simply the result of natural business acumen and that the efficiencies created by Standard Oil ultimately benefited consumers. Despite this defense, public sentiment continued to shift, with many Americans viewing Rockefeller's monopolistic control as a symbol of the growing gap between the rich and poor.

The Public Perception and the Role of Philanthropy

While Standard Oil's success was undeniable, it also generated considerable public backlash. Critics, especially muckraking journalists, painted Rockefeller as a ruthless monopolist who used unfair tactics to suppress competition and enrich himself at the expense of the public. The publication of Ida Tarbell's exposé, "The History of the Standard Oil Company," in 1904 highlighted the company's aggressive tactics and monopoly power, fueling anti-Rockefeller sentiment across the nation.

In response to the mounting criticism, Rockefeller began to pivot his public image. While his business practices remained largely unchanged, he began to focus more on philanthropy, and by the turn of the 20th century, he had begun to make significant charitable donations. These philanthropic efforts were aimed at improving his public image and counteracting some of the criticism directed at him and his company. Rockefeller's foundation efforts would go on to become a key aspect of his legacy, and he contributed millions of dollars to causes such as public health, education, and scientific research.

Despite his philanthropic activities, Standard Oil's dominance continued to be a point of contention. Public calls for antitrust reform grew louder as the company continued to control virtually every aspect of the oil industry in the United States. The growing pressure to break up Standard Oil would ultimately lead to a landmark antitrust case in 1911.

The Death of John D. Rockefeller and the Legacy of Standard Oil

John D. Rockefeller's life was one of remarkable achievements, but it was also one that had significant challenges, especially as he faced increasing public criticism for his monopolistic practices. Despite the controversies surrounding his wealth and business methods, Rockefeller's influence on both the oil industry and philanthropy was undeniable. As his empire continued to expand, so did his wealth, and with it, his increasing involvement in charitable activities.

Rockefeller's personal life took a turn toward introspection in his later years. While his business practices had helped create an industrial giant, the public opposition to Standard Oil and its monopolistic behavior was mounting. For much of his later life, Rockefeller was involved in philanthropy, focusing his energy on giving back to society and using his vast fortune to fund causes that he felt would have a lasting, positive impact. He became known as one of the world's most significant philanthropists, particularly for his work in public health, education, and scientific research.

Rockefeller's Later Years and Philanthropy

Rockefeller's transition from the head of Standard Oil to a philanthropist is a significant part of his legacy. Beginning in the 1880s and accelerating into the 20th century, Rockefeller began to shift his focus from business to charitable endeavors. He established the Rockefeller Foundation in 1913, which became one of the largest charitable organizations in the world. The foundation was particularly focused on promoting public health, medical research, and the advancement of education. Through his philanthropic work, Rockefeller sought to counterbalance some of the negative perceptions surrounding his business practices.

Rockefeller's contributions to education included major donations to universities such as the University of Chicago, which he founded in 1890. He also contributed to the development of scientific research, including the funding of medical research and the establishment of the Rockefeller Institute for Medical Research (now Rockefeller University), which became a world leader in medical and scientific breakthroughs.

Through these efforts, Rockefeller sought to leave a legacy that was about more than just oil and business. He believed that his wealth should be used to improve the lives of others, particularly in the areas of health, education, and social welfare.

The Breaking of Standard Oil and the Final Years of Rockefeller's Business Life

As the 20th century progressed, Standard Oil continued to be the subject of legal scrutiny and government action. In 1911, the U.S. Supreme Court ruled that Standard Oil's monopoly was in violation of the Sherman Antitrust Act, and it ordered the company to be broken up into 34 smaller, independent companies. While this decision was a major blow to Rockefeller's empire, it did not diminish his wealth. In fact, the breakup of Standard Oil's various entities actually led to an increase in Rockefeller's wealth, as the stocks of the companies were distributed to shareholders, including Rockefeller himself. Many of the companies that emerged from the breakup, including Exxon, Mobil, Chevron, and Amoco, would go on to become giants in the oil industry.

By this time, Rockefeller had largely stepped away from the daily operations of Standard Oil. He was focused on his philanthropic endeavors, spending his time supporting causes that would ensure a better future for humanity. Despite the legal defeat and the breakup of Standard Oil, Rockefeller's wealth continued to grow, thanks to his investments and his role as a major shareholder in many of the companies that resulted from the dissolution of the trust.

John D. Rockefeller's Death

John D. Rockefeller passed away on May 23, 1937, at the age of 97. His death marked the end of an era, not only for the oil industry but also for the American business world as a whole. At the time of his death, Rockefeller was the richest man in the world, with a fortune estimated to be around $1.4 billion, a sum that would be worth approximately $30 billion in today's dollars when adjusted for inflation.

His death was met with an outpouring of tributes from around the world, acknowledging his significant contributions to the business world and his charitable efforts. Despite the controversies of his early business career, many recognized his efforts to contribute positively to society through his philanthropy.

Following his passing, Rockefeller's legacy lived on through his charitable foundations, which continued to support research and social welfare programs for decades. The Rockefeller Foundation, in particular, became one of the world's most influential philanthropic organizations. The University of Chicago, which he had supported throughout his life, remains one of the world's leading research universities. The Rockefeller Institute, which he founded, became a center for groundbreaking medical research and continues to make important contributions to science and medicine.

Legacy and Reflection on Rockefeller's Life

John D. Rockefeller's legacy is one that is still debated and discussed today. On one hand, he revolutionized the oil industry and established an empire that would go on to shape the course of American business history. On the other hand, his methods—particularly his monopoly-building strategies—raised ethical questions that are still relevant in today's discussions of corporate power and economic inequality.

Rockefeller's story is also a reflection of the changing landscape of American industry during the late 19th and early 20th centuries. The rapid industrialization of the country, the rise of corporate capitalism, and the formation of monopolies all took place during Rockefeller's lifetime, and his actions were both a reflection of these trends and a driving force behind them. Rockefeller's success was not just about building a company but about creating a new kind of corporate structure that would shape American business practices for generations to come.

However, Rockefeller's shift toward philanthropy was also an important part of his legacy. The charitable foundations he established set the standard for corporate philanthropy in the 20th century, and his personal donations helped to shape the fields of medicine, education, and scientific research. His philanthropic efforts not only helped to improve the lives of millions of people but also contributed to some of the greatest advances in science and public health during his time.

In the end, John D. Rockefeller was a man of contradictions—both a symbol of the potential for individual success and a reminder of the dangers of unchecked corporate power. His rise to power, his philanthropic work, and the controversy surrounding his monopoly practices make him one of the most complex figures in American history. His death in 1937 marked the end of an era, but his influence—through his wealth, his companies, and his philanthropic efforts—continues to resonate to this day.

"The most important thing for a young man is to establish a credit-a reputation, character"- John D. Rockefeller

(Current Condition of Standard Oil Successors)

Current Condition of Standard Oil Successors

After the dissolution of the Standard Oil Trust in 1911, its constituent companies emerged as dominant players in the global oil industry. Today, many of these companies, such as ExxonMobil, Chevron, ConocoPhillips, Marathon Petroleum, and Occidental Petroleum, have grown into global energy giants with vast reserves of oil and natural gas, significant refining capacity, and extensive distribution networks. However, the evolution of these companies has also been shaped by new challenges in the modern energy landscape, including the push for environmental sustainability, renewable energy, and changing market conditions. Below is a closer look at the current status of these companies, examining their market performance, business strategies, financial health, and commitment to sustainability.

1. ExxonMobil

ExxonMobil, as the largest descendant of Standard Oil, remains a dominant player in the global oil and gas industry. However, the company is facing significant challenges as the energy sector undergoes rapid transformations.

Market Standing: ExxonMobil remains one of the largest publicly traded oil companies in the world, with a market capitalization regularly ranking among the top ten global corporations. The company is involved in a wide range of activities within the oil industry, including upstream exploration and production, refining, and chemicals. It operates in over 60 countries and is a major player in both oil and natural gas markets.

Financial Health: As of 2024, ExxonMobil is financially strong, with substantial revenue generated from both high oil prices and the company's vast integrated operations. Despite the volatility in oil prices, ExxonMobil has proven its resilience by maintaining strong earnings. The company has focused on cost reduction, streamlining operations, and increasing shareholder returns through dividend payments and stock buybacks.

Environmental Commitments: ExxonMobil has faced increasing pressure to reduce its carbon footprint and invest in renewable energy. While the company has made some strides in diversifying into cleaner energy sources, such as biofuels, hydrogen, and carbon capture technologies, critics argue that ExxonMobil's efforts are insufficient. ExxonMobil has set ambitious targets to reduce its net greenhouse gas emissions intensity but still faces scrutiny for its reliance on fossil fuels, which makes up a large portion of its operations.

Future Outlook: ExxonMobil's long-term outlook depends heavily on its ability to navigate the transition to a low-carbon economy. The company has committed to increasing its investments in green technologies, including carbon capture, utilization, and storage (CCUS), as well as advancing its renewable energy portfolio. ExxonMobil's ability to adapt to the energy transition while maintaining its profitability in the traditional oil and gas sector will be critical in the coming decades.

2. Chevron

Chevron, one of the most prominent successors to Standard Oil, continues to be a major player in the global energy sector. Its operations span across a wide range of areas, from oil exploration to refining and marketing, and it is also investing significantly in renewable energy technologies.

Market Standing: Chevron is a global leader in the oil and gas industry, consistently ranking as one of the largest publicly traded oil companies. It operates in over 180 countries, focusing on both upstream oil production and downstream refining. Chevron has a significant market share in natural gas production and is also involved in the development of biofuels and renewable energy sources, such as solar and wind energy. It has strong positions in offshore drilling, particularly in the Gulf of Mexico and offshore Africa.

Financial Health: Chevron has been able to maintain strong financial performance, benefiting from rising oil prices in recent years. Like ExxonMobil, the company has a strong balance sheet, with ample cash flow generated from its integrated operations. Chevron is also known for its consistent dividends, which appeal to long-term investors. The company has focused on improving operational efficiency and cost reduction to weather periods of lower oil prices.

Environmental Commitments: Chevron has committed to reducing its carbon footprint and increasing its investment in low-carbon technologies. The company has made significant strides in carbon capture and storage (CCS) technology and is exploring the potential for green hydrogen, which could help reduce emissions from hard-to-decarbonize sectors. However, as with ExxonMobil, Chevron's efforts to transition to renewable energy have been criticized as slow and insufficient to meet the global climate goals.

Future Outlook: Chevron's future will depend on how it balances the demand for oil and gas with the shift toward renewable energy. The company has signaled its intention to reduce its carbon intensity and invest more heavily in cleaner energy, but its ability to fully transition will require significant investments and strategic adjustments. Chevron's role in the clean energy transition will likely be an ongoing challenge as global governments push for greater environmental responsibility.

3. ConocoPhillips

ConocoPhillips, another prominent successor of Standard Oil, has evolved into a leading exploration and production company with a significant presence in North America and other global markets. The company has been focused on maintaining its upstream operations while positioning itself for the evolving energy transition.

Market Standing: ConocoPhillips is one of the largest independent exploration and production companies in the world. It operates in various global regions, including the United States, Canada, the North Sea, and Australia, and has a significant market share in both oil and natural gas production. Unlike ExxonMobil and Chevron, ConocoPhillips has focused primarily on the upstream segment of the oil industry, which involves exploration, drilling, and production.

Financial Health: ConocoPhillips remains financially healthy, with a strong emphasis on maintaining a disciplined approach to capital expenditures and operational efficiency. The company has capitalized on higher oil prices in recent years, posting solid earnings and generating significant cash flow. ConocoPhillips is also known for its conservative approach to debt management and its commitment to returning capital to shareholders.

Environmental Commitments: ConocoPhillips has set ambitious goals to reduce its greenhouse gas emissions and increase its investment in sustainable energy. The company is exploring opportunities in carbon capture and storage and renewable energy, particularly in wind and solar. ConocoPhillips has also committed to achieving net-zero emissions by 2050 and is working toward increasing its portfolio of low-carbon technologies. However, its reliance on oil and gas production remains a concern in the face of growing environmental pressures.

Future Outlook: As a predominantly upstream-focused company, ConocoPhillips faces unique challenges in the transition to a low-carbon economy. While it has invested in carbon management technologies, its long-term future will depend on the company's ability to balance the continued demand for oil and gas with the growing pressure to reduce emissions. The company's transition strategy will likely center on its ability to diversify its energy portfolio and lead in sustainable energy technologies.

4. Marathon Petroleum

Marathon Petroleum, originally part of the Standard Oil family, is now one of the largest independent refining companies in the United States. Its operations are heavily focused on refining and marketing, as well as the transportation and storage of oil products.

Market Standing: Marathon Petroleum is a major player in the U.S. refining sector and has one of the largest refining capacities in the world. It operates a network of refineries across the United States and a robust network of retail locations. Marathon also produces a wide range of refined petroleum products, including gasoline, diesel, and jet fuel. The company is a significant player in the midstream and downstream sectors, focusing on refining, logistics, and marketing.

Financial Health: Marathon Petroleum has been financially successful, driven by its focus on refining and the transportation of petroleum products. The company has benefited from strong demand for gasoline and diesel, particularly in the post-pandemic recovery. Marathon has also been a consistent dividend payer, reflecting its robust financial health and stable cash flow.

Environmental Commitments: As a refining-focused company, Marathon Petroleum is under increasing pressure to address environmental concerns associated with the fossil fuel industry. While the company has implemented efficiency improvements and carbon capture technologies in its operations, it is still heavily reliant on petroleum refining. Marathon's commitment to sustainability is evolving, and it is beginning to explore renewable energy and lower-carbon technologies, although its transition is less advanced compared to companies with greater exposure to upstream production.

Future Outlook: Marathon Petroleum's future will be shaped by the demand for refined oil products and the global push for cleaner fuels. The company is well-positioned in the refining sector but faces ongoing challenges in responding to market shifts toward electric vehicles and alternative fuels. Marathon's ability to innovate in the renewable energy space, particularly in biofuels, will be crucial to its long-term success.

CHAPTER THREE

ANDREW CARNEGIE – CARNEGIE STEEL COMPANY

(History of Andrew Carnegie – Carnegie Steel Company)

Humble Beginnings in Scotland Andrew Carnegie, a name synonymous with the industrial boom of 19th-century America, was born on November 25, 1835, in Dunfermline, Scotland. His early years were marked by humble beginnings; his father, William Carnegie, was a skilled handloom weaver, while his mother, Margaret Carnegie, supported the family through shoemaking and small trade. The Industrial Revolution, which introduced mechanized looms and other technological advancements, devastated the weaving industry in Scotland, plunging many families, including the Carnegies, into poverty. This economic downturn prompted the family to seek better opportunities in the United States, leading to their emigration in 1848 to Allegheny, Pennsylvania.

Early Struggles and a Hunger for Learning Carnegie's education was limited due to financial constraints, but he possessed an insatiable appetite for learning. His mother, a guiding force in his life, emphasized the importance of hard work and resilience. At the age of 13, Carnegie began working as a bobbin boy in a cotton factory, earning a mere $1.20 per week. Despite the long, grueling hours, he was determined to improve his situation and spent his spare time reading and expanding his knowledge. He soon secured a position as a telegraph messenger boy, where his diligence and curiosity about the workings of the telegraph system set him apart.

The Start of a Promising Career By the age of 18, Carnegie's skills earned him a job as a telegraph operator at the Pennsylvania Railroad Company, a pivotal moment that would shape his future. He caught the eye of Thomas A. Scott, the superintendent of the Western Division of the railroad. Scott became Carnegie's mentor, teaching him valuable lessons in management, investment, and strategic thinking. Under Scott's tutelage, Carnegie climbed the ranks to become Scott's personal assistant and eventually the superintendent of the Western Division.

A Turning Point: The American Civil War The American Civil War marked a significant turning point for Carnegie. During the war, he played an essential role in managing military transportation and supply routes for the Union Army, which enhanced his organizational acumen and broadened his understanding of logistical operations. This experience solidified Carnegie's belief in the power of technology and infrastructure as drivers of national progress and personal success.

Initial Investments and Business Success Carnegie's first major financial success came through strategic investments. His initial investment of $500 in the Adams Express Company, akin to today's logistics companies, yielded handsome returns. Encouraged by his early gains, he continued to invest in various ventures, including the Woodruff Sleeping Car Company, which capitalized on the growing need for long-distance travel amenities.

The Birth of a Steel Empire In the 1860s, Carnegie turned his attention to the burgeoning steel industry, foreseeing its critical role in the expansion of the American infrastructure, particularly in railroads and construction. He established the Keystone Bridge Company, aiming to replace wooden bridges with stronger and more durable steel structures. This venture laid the foundation for his steel empire, but it was the construction of the J. Edgar Thomson Steel Works in 1875 that marked a transformative moment. Named after the president of the Pennsylvania Railroad, the facility was strategically located near Pittsburgh and employed the groundbreaking Bessemer process, which revolutionized steel production by reducing costs and increasing output.

Innovative Use of the Bessemer Process The Bessemer process, developed by Sir Henry Bessemer, involved blowing air through molten iron to remove impurities, significantly reducing the cost of production. Carnegie was among the first American industrialists to adopt this innovative method, which gave him a significant competitive advantage. The efficiency of the Bessemer process allowed Carnegie Steel to produce vast quantities of steel at a lower cost than his competitors, positioning the company as a dominant force in the industry. This strategic use of technology, combined with Carnegie's keen business insight, enabled him to undercut his rivals' prices and secure lucrative contracts for infrastructure projects across the United States.

Vertical Integration for Maximum Control Carnegie's business practices were defined by his commitment to vertical integration—a strategy that involved controlling every aspect of the production process, from raw material extraction to transportation and manufacturing. He acquired iron ore mines, coal fields, railroads, and shipping lines to ensure a steady supply of resources for his steel mills. This allowed him to minimize production costs, maintain consistent quality, and eliminate reliance on third-party suppliers. Such a model of comprehensive control helped Carnegie Steel maximize profits and solidify its dominance in the steel industry.

Dominance and Urban Growth The late 19th century saw unprecedented growth in urbanization and infrastructure, fueling the demand for steel. Skyscrapers, bridges, and railroads required strong, affordable materials, and Carnegie Steel met this demand with unmatched efficiency. The company's output was so substantial that by the 1890s, it produced more steel than all of Great Britain combined. This rapid expansion and success made Carnegie one of the wealthiest men of his time.

A Philanthropic Vision Despite his success, Carnegie's ambition was coupled with a belief in social responsibility. He famously articulated his philosophy in his essay "The Gospel of Wealth," published in 1889. In it, he argued that the wealthy had a moral obligation to distribute their wealth in ways that promoted the welfare and betterment of society. Carnegie's adherence to this principle was evident in his later years when he focused on philanthropic efforts, donating vast sums to establish libraries, educational institutions, and foundations that continue to benefit society today.

The Homestead Strike and Controversy However, Carnegie's road to success was not without controversy. Labor relations at Carnegie Steel were strained, particularly at the Homestead Steel Works. In 1892, tensions erupted into the infamous Homestead Strike, a violent conflict between steelworkers and the company's management. The strike arose over wage cuts and deteriorating working conditions and became a defining moment in labor history. While Carnegie himself was in Scotland during the strike, his partner, Henry Clay Frick, was in charge of handling the situation. Frick's decision to hire Pinkerton agents to break the strike led to a bloody confrontation that resulted in multiple deaths and injuries. The public reaction was mixed, and while Carnegie's reputation was somewhat tarnished, the company continued to thrive.

The Sale of Carnegie Steel By 1901, Carnegie decided to retire and sell his company. He negotiated the sale of Carnegie Steel to J.P. Morgan for $480 million—a staggering sum at the time, equivalent to billions today. This deal led to the formation of U.S. Steel, the world's first billion-dollar corporation. With his fortune secured, Carnegie dedicated the remainder of his life to philanthropy, funding the construction of over 2,500 libraries worldwide, supporting education through scholarships and endowments, and establishing the Carnegie Foundation, the Carnegie Institution for Science, and Carnegie Mellon University.

Global Influence and Lasting Impact Carnegie's influence extended far beyond the steel industry. His business practices, particularly vertical integration and the innovative use of technology, became models for modern industrial operations. Many of the principles he championed, such as the importance of infrastructure development, competition, and efficient resource management, shaped the growth of American industry in the 20th century and inspired future entrepreneurs and business leaders worldwide.

Philanthropy and the Modernization of Education Carnegie's focus on education marked a significant shift in the philanthropic landscape of his time. His donations helped create a new model for funding public services, particularly in the fields of libraries and education. The over 2,500 public libraries he funded across the world, particularly in the United States, provided communities with access to knowledge and learning that was previously unattainable for the working class. Carnegie believed that education was a key to societal progress, and his contributions helped democratize learning opportunities. His support for higher education institutions, such as the establishment of Carnegie Mellon University, continues to have a profound effect on research, technology, and innovation today.

Carnegie's Enduring Philosophy on Wealth and Society Carnegie's "Gospel of Wealth" philosophy, which argued that the rich should use their wealth to improve society, continues to influence modern discussions on wealth inequality and social responsibility. The idea that successful individuals should not merely accumulate wealth for personal gain but should actively contribute to the betterment of humanity resonates with the modern concept of corporate social responsibility. Carnegie's approach set the stage for a new wave of philanthropic engagement by wealthy individuals, paving the way for later philanthropists like John D. Rockefeller, Bill Gates, and Warren Buffett, who have similarly dedicated large portions of their wealth to global causes.

Carnegie's Role in the Labor Movement Despite his contributions to society, Carnegie's legacy in labor relations is complex. His role in the Homestead Strike has led to ongoing debates about the balance between business growth and worker welfare. While Carnegie promoted efficiency and technological innovation, his treatment of workers—especially in the steel mills—exemplified the darker side of industrialization. The strike, which resulted in violence and loss of life, highlighted the growing tensions between labor and capital during the industrial revolution. Although Carnegie's personal role in the event was limited, it remains a central chapter in understanding his complex legacy in labor rights and the development of the American industrial workforce.

Carnegie's Impact on the American Dream Andrew Carnegie's life story became a quintessential example of the American Dream. His rise from a poor Scottish immigrant to one of the wealthiest men in the world demonstrated the possibilities that America offered to those willing to work hard, innovate, and take risks. His success story resonated deeply with the immigrant experience, particularly for those seeking a better life in the United States. Carnegie's achievements helped shape the narrative of America as a land of opportunity, reinforcing the belief that anyone, regardless of their origins, could achieve greatness through perseverance and ambition.

The Carnegie Legacy in the 21st Century Today, Carnegie's legacy continues to shape American industry, philanthropy, and education. Institutions like Carnegie Mellon University and the Carnegie Corporation of New York carry forward his vision of making a meaningful difference in the world. Additionally, his philanthropic endeavors have inspired future generations of business leaders to consider the broader impact of their wealth. While the steel industry he helped build has evolved, the principles of innovation, philanthropy, and responsibility that Carnegie championed still resonate with entrepreneurs, educators, and philanthropists striving to leave a lasting positive mark on society.

Legacy and Final Years Andrew Carnegie passed away on August 11, 1919, at the age of 83. His legacy endures not only in the vast wealth he accumulated but also in his contributions to society through his philanthropy.

"The man who dies thus rich dies disgraced"-Andrew Carnegie

(The Rise of Andrew Carnegie and Carnegie Steel Company)

The Rise of Andrew Carnegie and Carnegie Steel Company

Andrew Carnegie's rise from a poor immigrant to one of the wealthiest industrialists in the world is a story of vision, perseverance, and innovation. His success was built on a keen understanding of business, strategic investments, and a relentless drive to expand his influence in key industries. The creation and expansion of Carnegie Steel Company, which dominated the American steel industry in the late 19th and early 20th centuries, exemplify how one man's determination transformed an entire industry and reshaped the American economy.

Early Career and Strategic Investments

Andrew Carnegie's rise can be attributed to his ability to recognize lucrative business opportunities early on. Born in Scotland in 1835, he immigrated to the United States with his family when he was just a child. Arriving in Pittsburgh, he started working at a young age, taking on a variety of low-wage jobs. Despite his limited formal education, Carnegie was highly resourceful and taught himself by reading books in his free time.

One of his first major business opportunities came when he was employed as a messenger boy and later as a clerk at the Pennsylvania Railroad. Carnegie's work ethic and entrepreneurial spirit led him to take up side investments in the railroad industry. He started to buy stocks and eventually became an influential figure within the railroad sector. By the time he was in his mid-30s, he had accumulated enough wealth to transition into more significant ventures, including those in the steel industry.

Carnegie's early investments in the railroad and telegraph companies allowed him to build a financial foundation that would eventually fund his acquisition of steel-related ventures. The Pennsylvania Railroad and other railroads were vital to the transportation of steel, and Carnegie recognized the interconnectedness between railroads and steel production. This early insight laid the groundwork for his future business empire.

The Formation of Carnegie Steel Company

The pivotal moment in Carnegie's industrial journey came in 1865 when he founded Carnegie Steel Company. At the time, steel production in the United States was still relatively inefficient, relying on outdated methods such as the blast furnace. However, new advancements in steel manufacturing, particularly the Bessemer process, presented an opportunity to produce steel more efficiently and at a lower cost.

Carnegie was quick to see the potential of these new technologies. In 1875, he built the Edgar Thomson Steel Works in Braddock, Pennsylvania, which became the cornerstone of his steel empire. The plant utilized the Bessemer process, a revolutionary method of converting iron into steel using oxygen to remove impurities. This innovation enabled Carnegie Steel to produce large quantities of steel at a fraction of the previous cost. Carnegie was also an early adopter of the open-hearth process, which further improved the quality and efficiency of steel production.

Carnegie's commitment to technological innovation did not stop with the adoption of the Bessemer process. He continuously reinvested in new machinery, equipment, and facilities to improve production. The success of the Edgar Thomson Steel Works marked a turning point in Carnegie's career. It allowed him to transition from a small-scale producer to a leading figure in the steel industry, as his mills could now produce steel on an industrial scale.

Vertical Integration: A Game-Changer for Carnegie

A key strategy in Carnegie's rise was his commitment to vertical integration, a business model where a company controls every aspect of the production process. Carnegie understood that in order to achieve maximum efficiency and minimize costs, he needed to control the supply chain from start to finish.

In the early years of his steel production, Carnegie invested heavily in acquiring the raw materials needed for steel manufacturing. He purchased iron ore mines, coal mines, and limestone quarries, securing the supply of essential raw materials. This allowed him to reduce reliance on external suppliers and lower the costs of production. Carnegie's investment in transportation infrastructure, including railroads and shipping lines, further solidified his control over the entire production and distribution process.

By the late 1880s, Carnegie Steel had become the largest and most efficient steel producer in the United States. Carnegie's vertical integration strategy not only allowed his company to dominate the steel industry, but it also helped reduce costs, improve quality, and increase production capacity. As a result, Carnegie Steel was able to offer its products at competitive prices, which ultimately drove out smaller competitors.

Expanding the Steel Empire

As Carnegie's wealth and influence grew, so did his ambitions. His success was not just about acquiring raw materials or controlling the production process, but about constantly expanding the scale of his operations. Carnegie believed in economies of scale—the idea that the more steel his company produced, the cheaper and more efficient the process would become. This belief drove him to continue expanding his steel mills and increasing production capacity.

One of Carnegie's most significant moves in this direction came in 1892, when he consolidated his holdings into the Carnegie Steel Company. This merger brought together all of his steel mills and related businesses under one umbrella, creating a streamlined operation that could produce steel more efficiently than any other company in the world. By this point, Carnegie Steel controlled a significant portion of the U.S. steel industry, and Carnegie himself was regarded as the wealthiest industrialist in the country.

Carnegie's steel mills were some of the largest and most technologically advanced in the world. His facilities were known for their cutting-edge machinery, efficient production methods, and high-quality steel. His ability to produce steel at such a large scale and at such a low cost allowed Carnegie to dominate the steel market and make significant inroads into global markets.

The Role of Innovation and Efficiency

One of the key factors behind the rise of Carnegie Steel was its emphasis on innovation and efficiency. Carnegie was constantly seeking ways to improve the production process, reduce waste, and increase output. His focus on efficiency was reflected in the operation of his mills, which were some of the most advanced in the world. Carnegie invested in the latest technology, machinery, and methods, ensuring that his company remained at the forefront of the steel industry.

In addition to technological advancements, Carnegie understood the importance of management and organization in running an efficient business. He surrounded himself with talented managers and engineers who shared his vision for a more efficient and profitable steel production process. One of Carnegie's key managerial philosophies was to create a system where workers were incentivized to be more productive. Carnegie often offered performance bonuses and pay raises to employees who contributed to the company's success, which helped to foster a culture of hard work and innovation within his steel mills.

The Impact of the Homestead Strike

Despite his business acumen and the success of Carnegie Steel, Carnegie's rise was not without controversy. The company's treatment of workers, particularly during the Homestead Strike of 1892, tarnished Carnegie's reputation. The strike occurred when workers at Carnegie's Homestead Steel Works in Pennsylvania went on strike in protest of wage cuts and poor working conditions. Carnegie's manager, Henry Clay Frick, responded to the strike by bringing in armed Pinkerton agents to break the strike, leading to violent clashes and several deaths.

Although Carnegie was in Scotland during the strike and tried to distance himself from the violence, his reputation as a philanthropist and industrialist was damaged. The strike highlighted the harsh working conditions and the growing tensions between labor and management in the steel industry. Despite this, Carnegie continued to push forward with his business operations, and by the end of the 19th century, his company had become the largest steel producer in the world.

The Sale of Carnegie Steel and the Legacy of Andrew Carnegie

By 1901, Carnegie had reached the height of his industrial career. The company had grown to such a size that it was no longer manageable for one man. In 1901, Carnegie made the decision to sell Carnegie Steel to J.P. Morgan for $480 million, a deal that made him one of the richest men in the world. This sale marked the end of Carnegie's direct involvement in the steel industry, but his legacy as a titan of American industry was already cemented.

After selling his steel company, Carnegie turned his attention to philanthropy. He dedicated the rest of his life to giving away the vast majority of his fortune, funding libraries, educational institutions, and cultural organizations. Carnegie's philanthropic efforts were guided by his belief in the "Gospel of Wealth," the idea that the wealthy had a moral obligation to use their fortunes for the greater good of society.

The Legacy of Carnegie's Philanthropy

After selling Carnegie Steel to J.P. Morgan in 1901, Andrew Carnegie shifted his focus from amassing wealth to philanthropy, marking the next chapter in his life. His belief in the "Gospel of Wealth," articulated in an 1889 article, emphasized that the wealthy should not hoard their riches but instead invest in the public good, leaving a lasting impact on society. Carnegie argued that wealth should be used for the betterment of society, and he set out to do just that by donating his fortune to various causes.

In the years following the sale of Carnegie Steel, Carnegie donated an estimated $350 million of his fortune (around 90% of his wealth) to build institutions that would serve the public interest. His donations helped fund libraries, educational institutions, scientific research, and cultural organizations. Carnegie's approach was not simply to give away money but to fund institutions that would empower individuals and communities to thrive long after his death.

The Carnegie Libraries

One of the most significant aspects of Carnegie's philanthropic legacy was his commitment to building libraries across the United States and around the world. By the time of his death in 1919, Carnegie had funded the construction of over 2,500 libraries in the U.S. and several hundred more internationally. His passion for libraries stemmed from his belief in the power of knowledge to elevate individuals and communities. Carnegie argued that libraries were tools for social mobility, providing people with access to knowledge and opportunities for self-improvement.

Carnegie's philosophy behind the library movement was clear: he wanted to ensure that anyone, regardless of their background, had the opportunity to improve themselves through access to literature and educational materials. His foundation funded libraries in cities and towns across the country, and many of these libraries continue to serve as cultural and educational hubs today.

Educational and Cultural Investments

Carnegie's commitment to education was also evident in his funding of institutions of higher learning. One of his most famous donations was the creation of Carnegie Mellon University in Pittsburgh, a world-renowned institution for science, technology, and the arts. He also donated large sums of money to support other educational institutions, including the University of Edinburgh and the Carnegie Institute of Technology, among many others.

Carnegie believed that education was the key to social progress and individual empowerment. By investing in educational institutions, he hoped to provide future generations with the tools needed to succeed in a rapidly changing world. In addition to supporting formal education, Carnegie also contributed to the arts and sciences, funding museums, concert halls, and research facilities.

The Carnegie Corporation of New York

In 1911, Carnegie established the Carnegie Corporation of New York, which aimed to promote the advancement of knowledge and education. The Corporation's mandate was broad, and it supported a wide range of initiatives, including the establishment of schools, the promotion of scientific research, and the advancement of international peace. It also funded programs focused on public health, social welfare, and democracy.

The Carnegie Corporation is still active today, continuing to support projects in education, international peace, and science. The philanthropic organization carries on Carnegie's vision of improving society through investment in public institutions and services.

Carnegie's Influence on American Industry and the Global Economy

Beyond his philanthropic efforts, Carnegie's rise to prominence and the success of Carnegie Steel had a profound effect on the American industrial landscape and the global economy. As the largest steel producer in the United States, Carnegie Steel played a key role in the development of modern infrastructure, including bridges, railroads, and buildings, which were the backbone of the rapidly industrializing nation.

The steel produced by Carnegie Steel was essential in the construction of landmarks such as the Brooklyn Bridge and the skyscrapers that defined America's emerging skyline. The widespread availability of cheap, high-quality steel allowed industries across the U.S. to expand rapidly, leading to the creation of more jobs and the growth of major cities.

At a global level, Carnegie's business practices helped shape the future of capitalism. His commitment to innovation, cost reduction, and vertical integration became a model for future industrialists. The success of Carnegie Steel and the dominance of the company in the steel industry contributed to the rise of other industrial giants, including those in railroads, manufacturing, and oil. Carnegie's influence helped fuel the second phase of the Industrial Revolution, which saw the expansion of consumer goods, mass production, and the creation of new technologies.

Carnegie's Role in Shaping Labor Relations

While Carnegie's business practices and investments in technology revolutionized the steel industry, they also exposed the growing divide between industrialists and labor. The rise of Carnegie Steel was marked by repeated labor strikes, particularly as the company expanded and modernized its facilities. One of the most infamous of these was the Homestead Strike of 1892, which pitted the steel workers against Carnegie's management.

The Homestead Strike was a turning point in the history of labor relations in the United States. Carnegie's management, under the direction of Henry Clay Frick, responded to the strike with force, bringing in the Pinkerton National Detective Agency to break the strike. This led to violent clashes between the strikers and the agents, resulting in several deaths and injuries.

Though Carnegie was not directly involved in the violence—he was in Scotland at the time—the strike tarnished his reputation as a philanthropist and reformer. The brutal crackdown on workers and the subsequent public outcry highlighted the harsh conditions under which industrial workers labored in the late 19th century. It also marked a significant moment in the labor movement, as it underscored the need for better working conditions, fair wages, and improved labor rights.

Despite the controversies surrounding labor disputes, Carnegie continued to emphasize the importance of both labor and capital in the success of his business. His approach to management, which was focused on efficiency, cost control, and innovation, did not necessarily align with the demands of workers. However, it was clear that his contributions to the industry as a whole were transformative, even if the treatment of workers was less than ideal.

Carnegie's Influence on Corporate America

Carnegie's impact on corporate America extends beyond his contributions to the steel industry. He was a pioneer in creating large, vertically integrated companies, a model that would become standard practice in many industries. By controlling all aspects of production, from raw materials to finished goods, Carnegie was able to maintain control over quality, cost, and supply.

His management style, though at times contentious, also helped establish a culture of efficiency and innovation. Carnegie's focus on reinvesting profits into his business and constantly seeking ways to reduce costs and improve productivity helped shape the modern corporate world. His success served as a template for other business magnates, including John D. Rockefeller in oil and J.P. Morgan in finance.

Carnegie's experience also helped lay the foundation for the modern American corporation. The creation of Carnegie Steel set a precedent for mergers and acquisitions, as the company was eventually consolidated with other steel firms to form U.S. Steel in 1901. This merger was led by J.P. Morgan and became the world's first billion-dollar corporation. The rise of U.S. Steel symbolized the culmination of the industrial revolution and the emergence of corporate giants that would dominate the global economy for much of the 20th century.

Andrew Carnegie's Final Years and Legacy

Andrew Carnegie retired from the steel industry in 1901, but his legacy continued to shape both the American economy and philanthropic practices for decades to come. After his sale of Carnegie Steel, he focused his attention on giving away his wealth, and his legacy as one of the greatest philanthropists in history endures today.

Carnegie's commitment to philanthropy has left a lasting imprint on American society. His contributions to education, libraries, and cultural institutions have had an enduring impact on the development of American intellectual and cultural life. Carnegie's work in the field of philanthropy has inspired generations of wealthy individuals to dedicate their resources to causes that benefit society, and his influence can still be seen in the numerous institutions that bear his name.

Though his business practices were at times controversial and his labor relations were criticized, Andrew Carnegie's rise from humble beginnings to industrial titan is a testament to the power of ambition, innovation, and hard work. His legacy in steel, philanthropy, and corporate management continues to influence the fields of business and philanthropy today, making him one of the most important figures in American history.

(Current Status of Carnegie Steel Company)

The Carnegie Steel Company, once the dominant force in the steel industry, no longer exists under its original name or structure. However, the legacy of Andrew Carnegie's company lives on through the modern steel conglomerates that evolved from it. The company itself was sold in 1901 to J.P. Morgan, who merged it with several other steel companies to form U.S. Steel, which remains one of the largest steel manufacturers in the world today. The transformation of Carnegie Steel into U.S. Steel marks the end of an era and the beginning of a new chapter in the American industrial landscape.

This article will explore the legacy and current condition of Carnegie Steel's successor, U.S. Steel, the company formed from the merger of Carnegie's steel empire, and how it has adapted to the changes in the global steel industry over the last century.

The Birth of U.S. Steel

In 1901, J.P. Morgan orchestrated the merger of Carnegie Steel with several other steel companies, including the Federal Steel Company and the National Steel Company. This consolidation formed U.S. Steel, the first billion-dollar corporation in history. The creation of U.S. Steel was a monumental moment in industrial history, reflecting the rapid consolidation of American business in the late 19th and early 20th centuries.

At the time of the merger, U.S. Steel controlled more than two-thirds of the steel production in the United States, cementing its position as the largest steel manufacturer in the world. Under the leadership of J.P. Morgan and the continued influence of Carnegie's principles, the company expanded its reach, modernized its facilities, and became the backbone of American industry.

Despite Carnegie's departure from the day-to-day operations after the sale of his company, his innovations in steel manufacturing and business practices continued to shape U.S. Steel's operations. The company adopted Carnegie's principles of vertical integration, which involved controlling every aspect of the production process, from raw materials to finished steel. This structure allowed U.S. Steel to produce steel more efficiently and at lower costs than many of its competitors.

U.S. Steel's Growth and Challenges in the 20th Century

U.S. Steel dominated the steel industry for much of the 20th century. The company expanded its operations internationally, establishing steel mills and plants in countries around the world. It played a crucial role in the growth of the U.S. economy, providing the steel necessary for infrastructure projects, war efforts, and industrial growth. The steel produced by U.S. Steel was used in everything from railroads and skyscrapers to military vehicles and ships.

However, despite its dominance, U.S. Steel faced significant challenges throughout the 20th century. The company's size and structure made it less flexible in adapting to changes in the market. As new technologies emerged and foreign competitors began to offer lower-cost steel, U.S. Steel struggled to maintain its competitive edge. The company was slow to adopt newer, more efficient production methods, such as electric arc furnaces, which would later become a standard in the steel industry.

Throughout the mid-20th century, U.S. Steel faced increasing pressure from labor unions, particularly during the post-war period when workers began to demand higher wages and better working conditions. The company's labor relations were often contentious, as steelworkers pushed for improved benefits and job security. In the 1970s and 1980s, U.S. Steel's market share began to decline as new competitors entered the market, both domestic and foreign. The company's inability to keep pace with technological advancements and its outdated infrastructure contributed to its struggles during this period.

The Decline of the American Steel Industry

The decline of U.S. Steel mirrored the broader challenges faced by the American steel industry in the latter half of the 20th century. As global competition intensified, U.S. Steel, along with many of its peers, began to lose ground to foreign producers, particularly those in Japan and Europe, which had adopted more modern production techniques.

In the 1970s and 1980s, many U.S. steel mills were operating with outdated equipment, while foreign mills had embraced new technologies, such as mini-mills, which used electric arc furnaces to recycle scrap steel into new products. These mini-mills were more cost-effective and environmentally friendly than traditional blast furnaces, which required large amounts of raw materials and energy.

The U.S. steel industry also faced a decline in demand during this period, as American manufacturing began to move overseas, and the global economy shifted towards more service-oriented industries. By the 1980s, U.S. Steel had begun to reduce its workforce, close plants, and consolidate operations. The company's once-dominant position in the market had eroded, and it was no longer the behemoth it had been in the early 20th century.

U.S. Steel Today: A Changing Landscape

Today, U.S. Steel is no longer the dominant player in the steel industry that it once was. The company's market share has been reduced, and its influence in the global steel market has diminished. However, it remains one of the largest steel manufacturers in the United States and is still an important player in the global steel market.

In recent years, U.S. Steel has faced a number of challenges, both internal and external, as the company has struggled to maintain profitability in an increasingly competitive market. The company's operations are now more focused on producing high-quality steel products, such as steel for automobiles, construction, and energy infrastructure, rather than the mass production of basic steel.

Financial Challenges and Restructuring

U.S. Steel has faced ongoing financial challenges in the 21st century. In recent years, the company has experienced fluctuating profits, often tied to global steel prices, which are subject to supply and demand fluctuations. The company has also struggled with its legacy costs, including pension obligations and healthcare benefits for retired workers. As part of its efforts to address these financial difficulties, U.S. Steel has engaged in restructuring efforts, including the closure of outdated facilities, the sale of non-core assets, and the reduction of its workforce.

Despite these challenges, U.S. Steel remains a significant player in the American steel industry. The company operates several large steel mills in the U.S., including its flagship plant in Gary, Indiana, which remains one of the largest steel mills in the world. U.S. Steel also has operations in Canada, and it is involved in joint ventures with foreign companies in countries such as Serbia and Brazil.

Technological Advancements and Innovation

In an effort to stay competitive, U.S. Steel has invested heavily in new technologies. The company has implemented advanced manufacturing processes, such as continuous casting, which allows for more efficient production of steel. U.S. Steel has also made efforts to reduce its environmental impact by improving energy efficiency and reducing emissions from its steel mills. The company has partnered with several organizations to explore new technologies, such as carbon capture and storage (CCS), to reduce its carbon footprint and address the challenges of climate change.

In 2020, U.S. Steel announced plans to invest $1.5 billion in the development of a new, state-of-the-art steel plant in Arkansas. The new plant will use electric arc furnaces, which are more environmentally friendly and cost-efficient than traditional blast furnaces. This investment is part of the company's broader strategy to modernize its facilities and improve its competitiveness in the global steel market.

U.S. Steel has also embraced digital technologies, such as artificial intelligence and automation, to improve its manufacturing processes. The company is exploring the use of machine learning and predictive analytics to optimize production and reduce costs. These advancements will help U.S. Steel remain competitive in an industry that is increasingly focused on efficiency and sustainability.

U.S. Steel's Role in the Global Steel Market

Despite its challenges, U.S. Steel remains an important player in the global steel market. The company continues to produce a wide range of steel products for industries such as automotive, energy, and construction. U.S. Steel's steel is used in the production of everything from skyscrapers to energy infrastructure to automobiles, making it a crucial part of the global economy.

However, U.S. Steel faces increasing competition from both foreign producers and domestic mini-mills. The rise of mini-mills, which are smaller, more flexible steel producers, has made it more difficult for traditional steel giants like U.S. Steel to maintain their dominance in the market. Mini-mills have lower overhead costs and are able to respond more quickly to market fluctuations, giving them a competitive edge.

At the same time, U.S. Steel's reliance on its large, integrated mills has left it vulnerable to shifts in the global steel market. The company's reliance on steel production from traditional blast furnaces, while still significant, has led to higher production costs compared to mini-mills and other modern steel manufacturers.

U.S. Steel's Future: Sustainability and Innovation

Looking forward, U.S. Steel's future is heavily tied to the ongoing evolution of the steel industry and the need for greater sustainability. Steel production is one of the most carbon-intensive industries in the world, and U.S. Steel has been under increasing pressure from both the public and regulatory bodies to reduce its environmental impact.

In response to this challenge, U.S. Steel has made a concerted effort to improve its sustainability practices. The company is exploring the use of renewable energy sources, such as wind and solar, to power its operations. It has also committed to reducing its greenhouse gas emissions in line with the goals of the Paris Agreement.

To remain competitive, U.S. Steel will need to continue investing in technological advancements, including carbon capture technologies, electric arc furnaces, and automation. The company's ability to adapt to the changing global market and the increasing emphasis on sustainability will play a crucial role in its long-term success.

Additionally, U.S. Steel's ability to maintain its domestic market share in the face of global competition will be critical. While the company remains a major player in the U.S., it will need to continue innovating and streamlining its operations to compete with lower-cost producers from countries like China, India, and South Korea.

CHAPTER FOUR

WALT DISNEY-THE WALT DISNEY COMPANY

(History of Walt Disney and The Walt Disney Company)

The History of Walt Disney and The Walt Disney Company

The story of Walt Disney and his company is one of the most remarkable in the history of entertainment. What started as a modest animation studio founded by an ambitious visionary, Walt Disney, has since grown into one of the largest, most influential entertainment conglomerates in the world. The Walt Disney Company, commonly referred to as Disney, encompasses a diverse range of media and entertainment properties, including movies, television, theme parks, and a vast array of consumer products.

Walt Disney's rise to fame and the transformation of his company is an inspiring tale of creativity, innovation, and perseverance. Through a series of groundbreaking accomplishments, Disney's influence on global culture has been immense. In this article, we will trace the origins of Walt Disney, the founding and growth of The Walt Disney Company, and its evolution into the media powerhouse it is today.

Early Life of Walt Disney

Walt Disney was born on December 5, 1901, in Chicago, Illinois, to Elias Disney and Flora Call Disney. Walt's early life was marked by both financial struggles and a passion for drawing. The Disney family moved frequently, eventually settling in Kansas City, Missouri, where Walt attended school. Walt's artistic inclinations were clear early on, as he began drawing sketches and selling them to neighbors. He was also captivated by the world of animation, and it was during his time in Kansas City that he discovered the magic of film.

In his teenage years, Disney attended the Kansas City Art Institute, and later, he worked as an apprentice at the Pesmen-Rubin Art Studio. However, his career trajectory took a significant turn when he joined the Red Cross during World War I, where he served in France as an ambulance driver. Upon his return, Disney pursued his dream of working in the entertainment industry, particularly in animation.

Early Animation Career

Walt Disney's first foray into animation began with his early work at the Kansas City Film Ad Company, where he produced commercial animations. However, these early ventures proved unsuccessful, leading him to move to Hollywood in 1923, where he established the Disney Brothers Studio with his brother Roy Disney. Walt's ambition was clear, but the road was not without its challenges.

In 1923, Walt Disney began working on his first series of animated short films called Oswald the Lucky Rabbit, which was produced under a contract with Universal Pictures. Oswald was an immediate success and helped Walt Disney gain recognition in the animation world. However, a crucial setback occurred when Disney lost the rights to Oswald due to a dispute with his distributor, Universal Pictures. This moment, though initially devastating, would lead Walt to one of the most pivotal moments in the history of animation.

Creation of Mickey Mouse

In the wake of losing Oswald, Walt Disney, undeterred by the setback, created a new character: Mickey Mouse. The creation of Mickey Mouse is often considered one of the most important events in animation history. In 1928, Walt and his team, including animator Ub Iwerks, brought the character to life in a short film called Steamboat Willie. What made Steamboat Willie so groundbreaking was that it was one of the first cartoons to feature synchronized sound, a revolutionary advancement at the time.

The success of Mickey Mouse was immediate and overwhelming. Audiences were captivated by the character's personality and charm, and Mickey quickly became the face of Disney. Over the following years, Mickey's popularity only grew, leading to the creation of a series of animated shorts and comic strips. Mickey Mouse became not just a cartoon character, but a cultural icon, establishing Walt Disney as a visionary in the world of animation.

The Formation of The Walt Disney Company

The creation of Mickey Mouse was not just a triumph in animation; it was the foundation for what would become The Walt Disney Company. In 1929, Walt and Roy Disney officially renamed their company to The Walt Disney Studios. With Mickey Mouse's success, Walt Disney was able to further expand his creative ambitions, pushing the boundaries of animation and storytelling.

Throughout the 1930s, Walt Disney and his team would continue to innovate, leading to the creation of new characters and advancing the medium of animation. The release of The Skeleton Dance (1929) marked Disney's first true experimental animation, exploring abstract designs and synchronization with music. Later, the company would produce The Silly Symphonies series, which was instrumental in expanding the scope of animated shorts and exploring new techniques in animation.

The Birth of Feature-Length Animation

The Disney studio's greatest achievement during the 1930s was the creation of the world's first full-length animated feature film, Snow White and the Seven Dwarfs (1937). The idea of a full-length animated feature was an enormous risk, as there had never been a feature-length animated film before. Critics doubted whether an audience would sit through a full-length cartoon, but Walt Disney's belief in the project never wavered. The film was a monumental success, both critically and commercially, and it solidified Disney's place in history as the pioneer of feature-length animation.

Snow White and the Seven Dwarfs marked the beginning of Disney's dominance in the animated feature film industry. Following its success, Disney produced a series of other animated classics, such as Pinocchio (1940), Fantasia (1940), Dumbo (1941), and Bambi (1942). These films would go on to become cultural landmarks, beloved by generations of viewers.

Expansion into New Territories

As the company grew, so did Walt Disney's ambitions. He sought to expand into new territories, both creatively and geographically. In the 1940s and 1950s, Disney focused on diversifying the company's ventures beyond animation. This era marked the beginning of Disney's involvement in television, theme parks, and live-action film production.

Walt Disney's introduction to television came with the popular TV program The Wonderful World of Disney (1954), which brought Disney's animated films and short stories to the small screen. This was the beginning of the company's long relationship with television, and it helped to solidify Disney's position as a household name.

In the 1950s, Walt Disney's most ambitious project yet came to life: Disneyland. Opened in 1955 in Anaheim, California, Disneyland was the world's first theme park that fully integrated Walt Disney's characters, stories, and experiences into an immersive environment. Disneyland was a revolutionary concept, and it forever changed the way people thought about entertainment. It introduced the world to themed attractions, immersive storytelling, and character interactions, all of which have since become integral aspects of the theme park industry.

The 1960s and Walt Disney's Legacy

During the 1960s, Walt Disney continued to lead the company with creative energy, despite facing personal and professional challenges. However, his sudden death in 1966 at the age of 65 marked a pivotal moment in the company's history. Walt's death left a significant void at Disney, and his vision and leadership were sorely missed.

After Walt's death, the leadership of The Walt Disney Company was passed on to his brother Roy Disney, who continued to guide the company through its difficult transition. Roy oversaw the completion of Disney World in Florida, which was unveiled in 1971. Disney World, a much larger and more expansive park than Disneyland, featured the Magic Kingdom, EPCOT (Experimental Prototype Community of Tomorrow), and later, other themed attractions. Disney World became a major success, further cementing Disney's position as a leader in the theme park industry.

The Walt Disney Company in the 1970s and 1980s

Following Roy Disney's death in 1971, leadership of The Walt Disney Company passed to a series of executives. The company continued to face challenges, particularly in terms of creativity and profitability. Disney's animation division, which had dominated the industry, faced difficulties as the industry as a whole began to shift. The company also began to experience a series of financial challenges, and in the 1980s, the company faced a period of stagnation.

In 1984, Michael Eisner was appointed as the CEO of The Walt Disney Company. Eisner's leadership would prove to be a turning point for the company, as he helped revitalize Disney and steer it back into financial success. Eisner was responsible for making bold moves that reshaped the company, such as diversifying its portfolio with the acquisition of new properties and expanding Disney's television and movie offerings.

Under Eisner's leadership, Disney acquired major properties, such as the American Broadcasting Company (ABC), and expanded its portfolio of entertainment assets to include the creation of new theme parks, including EPCOT Center, which later became Epcot at Walt Disney World. The company also became involved in producing animated films like The Little Mermaid (1989) and Beauty and the Beast (1991), which marked the beginning of Disney's Renaissance period.

The 1990s and 2000s: Disney Renaissance and Acquisitions

The 1990s marked the start of a renaissance period for The Walt Disney Company, thanks to a string of critically and commercially successful animated films, including Aladdin (1992), The Lion King (1994), and Mulan (1998). These films helped revitalize Disney's animation division and solidified its place as a leader in family entertainment.

In the late 1990s, Disney also made strategic acquisitions, such as the purchase of Pixar Animation Studios in 2006, Marvel Entertainment in 2009, and Lucasfilm in 2012. These acquisitions brought popular properties like Toy Story, Spider-Man, Iron Man, and Star Wars under the Disney umbrella, giving the company an even greater share of the entertainment market.

The Transition from Michael Eisner to Bob Iger

Michael Eisner's tenure at the helm of Disney was a period marked by significant transformations, including revitalizing the company's theme parks and animation division. However, by the early 2000s, questions about the company's future arose, especially concerning Eisner's leadership style and the direction of Disney. In 2005, after a prolonged period of shareholder dissatisfaction and internal issues, Michael Eisner stepped down from his role as CEO.

Bob Iger, who had been with Disney for decades, took over as CEO in 2005. Iger's leadership proved to be instrumental in reshaping Disney for the modern era. One of his first major moves was to reverse the company's declining image by refocusing on its core strength: storytelling. Iger also recognized that Disney needed to adapt to the growing digital landscape, where streaming services, online video, and digital content were taking center stage. Under Iger, Disney would embark on a series of transformative acquisitions and strategic partnerships that set the company on its path to becoming a global media giant.

Strategic Acquisitions Under Bob Iger

Iger's vision for Disney was to make it more than just a family-friendly entertainment brand — he wanted to position it as a leader in global media and content creation. One of his most pivotal strategies was acquiring other major entertainment companies, significantly expanding Disney's intellectual property portfolio.

Pixar Acquisition (2006)

In 2006, Disney acquired Pixar Animation Studios for $7.4 billion, a groundbreaking move that fused two of the most iconic animation studios in the world. Pixar, known for its cutting-edge animation techniques and successful franchises like Toy Story, Finding Nemo, and The Incredibles, was an ideal complement to Disney's animation division. The acquisition not only added valuable intellectual property to Disney's arsenal but also allowed Pixar's leadership, including John Lasseter, to play a critical role in Disney's creative development.

The Pixar acquisition allowed Disney to reinvigorate its animation department, leading to a new era of animated classics such as Up (2009), Toy Story 3 (2010), Frozen (2013), and Inside Out (2015). Pixar's technical innovations and storytelling expertise significantly enhanced Disney's creative output, resulting in both commercial success and critical acclaim.

Marvel Entertainment (2009)

In 2009, Disney made another landmark acquisition when it purchased Marvel Entertainment for $4 billion. Marvel, with its extensive library of iconic superhero characters, including Spider-Man, Iron Man, the Hulk, and the X-Men, added an entirely new dimension to Disney's intellectual property. This move was particularly strategic as it allowed Disney to tap into the highly lucrative comic book movie genre, which was becoming increasingly popular.

Under Disney's ownership, Marvel Studios created the Marvel Cinematic Universe (MCU), which became one of the most successful film franchises in history. The MCU, starting with Iron Man in 2008, has produced over 30 films and grossed billions at the global box office. The MCU's success proved that Disney could transcend its traditional family-friendly branding and become a dominant force in action and adventure films.

The MCU's influence extended beyond films. Disney integrated Marvel characters into its theme parks, merchandise, television programs, and other media platforms. The MCU also contributed significantly to the rise of superhero films, paving the way for an entire cinematic genre that would dominate the 2010s and beyond.

Lucasfilm Acquisition (2012)

In 2012, Disney acquired Lucasfilm, the company behind the Star Wars franchise, for an astonishing $4.05 billion. The acquisition of Lucasfilm gave Disney control over one of the most beloved and profitable franchises in film history. With the Star Wars universe's vast lore, characters, and merchandising potential, this acquisition was seen as another critical step in Disney's ambition to dominate the entertainment industry.

The Star Wars films released under Disney, beginning with Star Wars: The Force Awakens (2015), received widespread acclaim, and the franchise's expanded universe in television, books, and theme parks further enhanced Disney's influence. In addition to the films, Disney incorporated Star Wars into its theme parks, opening Star Wars: Galaxy's Edge at Disneyland and Walt Disney World.

21st Century Fox Acquisition (2019)

Perhaps the most significant acquisition during Iger's tenure came in 2019 when Disney acquired 21st Century Fox in a deal worth $71.3 billion. This acquisition gave Disney control of key assets, including Fox's film and television studios, its stake in Hulu, and the rights to major properties such as Avatar, The Simpsons, and X-Men. With this acquisition, Disney expanded its footprint in both the film industry and the streaming market, as Fox's assets bolstered Disney's presence in the rapidly growing on-demand content sector.

The deal also increased Disney's international reach, particularly in markets such as Europe and Asia. Furthermore, the acquisition provided Disney with a robust back catalog of television programming, including classic films and television shows, which proved valuable in bolstering its streaming service, Disney+.

Disney+ and the Streaming Wars

With the rise of streaming services such as Netflix, Amazon Prime, and Hulu, Disney recognized that the future of entertainment was digital. In 2019, Disney launched its own streaming platform, Disney+, with the goal of becoming a leader in the digital entertainment landscape.

Disney+ quickly became a major player in the streaming wars, offering an extensive library of Disney classics, Pixar films, Marvel films and TV shows, Star Wars content, and National Geographic programming. Disney's vast library, coupled with its strong brand recognition, enabled Disney+ to attract millions of subscribers within a short period. In 2020, Disney announced that Disney+ had reached 86 million subscribers worldwide — a major milestone that solidified its place as a top-tier streaming service.

Disney+'s growth was accelerated by its exclusive content offerings, including original shows like The Mandalorian (2019), WandaVision (2021), and Loki (2021). These shows, tied to popular franchises such as Star Wars and the MCU, helped the platform attract new subscribers and retain existing ones. Furthermore, the success of Disney+ positioned Disney as a direct competitor to other major streaming platforms.

Disney's Theme Parks and Global Expansion

Beyond its digital ventures, Disney's theme parks and resorts have remained a central component of the company's success. Following the opening of Disneyland in 1955 and the subsequent opening of Walt Disney World in 1971, Disney expanded its theme park empire globally. The company opened Disneyland Paris in 1992, Tokyo Disneyland in 1983, Hong Kong Disneyland in 2005, and Shanghai Disneyland in 2016, with each park contributing to Disney's global dominance in the leisure and entertainment industry.

Disney's theme parks remain at the forefront of the company's business operations, consistently attracting millions of visitors annually. The parks not only serve as destinations for entertainment but also as major sources of revenue, with guests spending money on tickets, hotels, dining, and merchandise. Disney has continued to innovate with new attractions, immersive experiences, and technology, such as the introduction of virtual queues and mobile apps that enhance the guest experience.

Corporate Leadership and Vision

Throughout its history, The Walt Disney Company has been shaped by visionary leaders who have pushed the boundaries of entertainment. Walt Disney's pioneering spirit established the foundation for the company, but it was the leadership of executives like Roy Disney, Michael Eisner, and Bob Iger that enabled the company to evolve into the multimedia conglomerate it is today.

Bob Iger, in particular, is credited with guiding Disney through a period of unprecedented growth and transformation. His strategy of acquiring other entertainment companies, expanding Disney's global reach, and embracing new technologies such as streaming has set Disney on a path for continued success in the digital era. Under his leadership, Disney also invested heavily in content creation, ensuring that the company's entertainment offerings remained fresh and relevant in an ever-changing marketplace.

In 2020, Bob Chapek succeeded Bob Iger as CEO, continuing the legacy of innovation and strategic expansion. Chapek's tenure, however, has been marked by the challenges posed by the COVID-19 pandemic, which severely impacted Disney's theme parks and resorts. Despite these challenges, Disney's ability to pivot and adapt to the digital landscape, including expanding its streaming services, has kept it on a growth trajectory.

Walt Disney passed away on December 15, 1966, at the age of 65, after a battle with lung cancer. His death marked the end of an era for The Walt Disney Company, but his legacy has lived on through the immense influence he had on the entertainment industry. Disney's vision for storytelling, creativity, and innovation laid the foundation for a company that would grow into one of the largest and most successful entertainment conglomerates in the world. His commitment to excellence, imagination, and pushing the boundaries of what was possible in film and theme parks continues to inspire generations of creators, ensuring that his impact is felt worldwide

(Rise of Walt Disney and The Walt Disney Company)

The Rise of Walt Disney and The Walt Disney Company

The rise of Walt Disney and The Walt Disney Company is a story of entrepreneurial vision, creativity, and strategic expansion. From a young man with a dream in a small garage in Hollywood to the creation of one of the most influential and diverse entertainment empires in the world, Walt Disney's journey was built upon the principles of innovation, storytelling, and the pursuit of excellence.

The Beginning: A Dream and a Mouse

Walt Disney's rise began in the early 1920s when he moved to Hollywood, California, with his brother Roy. Together, they founded the Disney Brothers Studio in 1923, marking the formal inception of the Disney empire. The company initially struggled to find its footing, producing short films and other small projects with limited success. However, in 1928, Disney hit upon a transformative idea: the creation of Mickey Mouse.

Mickey Mouse, introduced in Steamboat Willie, was the first animated character to appear with synchronized sound. This innovation resonated with audiences and quickly made Mickey a star, capturing the hearts of children and adults alike. It was a major breakthrough, and in a short time, Mickey Mouse became one of the most recognizable and beloved characters in entertainment history. This moment is seen as the foundation for The Walt Disney Company's rise, as it brought both artistic recognition and commercial success.

The Success of Animated Feature Films

By the 1930s, Walt Disney had established himself as a major player in the animation industry. Building on the success of Mickey Mouse, Disney pushed the boundaries of animation with the release of Snow White and the Seven Dwarfs in 1937. It was the first full-length cel-animated feature film, and it marked a turning point in the industry.

Despite initial skepticism about the viability of animated feature films, Snow White proved to be a massive success, both financially and critically. The film's success demonstrated that animation could be a serious and profitable art form, helping to solidify Disney's reputation as a visionary in the field. Following this achievement, Walt Disney continued to innovate with other classic animated films such as Pinocchio, Fantasia, Dumbo, and Bambi—all of which pushed the limits of animation technology and storytelling.

Expansion into New Ventures: Theme Parks and Television

In the 1950s, Walt Disney saw an opportunity to expand his empire beyond animation. Recognizing the power of creating fully immersive experiences for families, Walt Disney opened Disneyland in 1955. Disneyland was the first-ever theme park that allowed visitors to interact with Disney characters, experience the magic of the movies, and enter into an entirely new world of fantasy. The park's opening was a groundbreaking event in the entertainment industry, and Disneyland quickly became one of the most visited attractions in the world.

The success of Disneyland set the stage for more parks, and in 1971, Walt Disney World opened in Florida. This massive resort complex featured multiple theme parks, hotels, and recreational facilities, and it would go on to become a global tourism icon. These parks, along with others opened later in Tokyo, Paris, Hong Kong, and Shanghai, would become key pillars of the company's business, making Disney a leader in global entertainment and tourism.

In addition to theme parks, Disney also ventured into television. In 1954, Walt Disney created The Wonderful World of Disney, a television program that showcased Disney movies and cartoons. It was an early effort by Disney to engage with audiences beyond the cinema, and it helped to grow the company's brand even further.

The Rise of The Walt Disney Company in the 1980s and 1990s

After Walt Disney's death in 1966, the company underwent significant changes, but the Disney spirit of innovation and creativity remained intact. Under the leadership of Roy Disney and, later, Michael Eisner, The Walt Disney Company entered a new era of growth in the 1980s and 1990s.

Eisner, who became CEO in 1984, played a pivotal role in revitalizing the company. He spearheaded the creation of new theme parks, including Disney-MGM Studios (now Disney's Hollywood Studios) in 1989, and helped expand Disney's presence in television with the launch of The Disney Channel in 1983. Disney's television division also became a major force, with shows like DuckTales and The Simpsons drawing millions of viewers.

During this period, Disney also began acquiring other entertainment companies to expand its portfolio. One of the most notable acquisitions was the purchase of Pixar Animation Studios in 2006 for $7.4 billion. Pixar was responsible for creating iconic films like Toy Story and Finding Nemo, and its acquisition allowed Disney to dominate the animated film industry, further strengthening its position in the entertainment world.

Expansion into New Markets: Film Studios and Acquisitions

The success of Disney's animated films, television shows, and theme parks was only part of the company's rise. In the 1990s, Disney also started making significant acquisitions in other entertainment sectors. The company acquired ABC and its affiliated networks, including ESPN, in 1995, giving it a powerful foothold in the television and sports entertainment markets.

In 2006, Disney's acquisition of Pixar Animation Studios allowed the company to cement its dominance in the animation space. Pixar had already revolutionized the animation industry with its groundbreaking CGI films, and its partnership with Disney allowed both companies to create blockbuster films that would become cultural milestones. Films like Toy Story 3, Monsters, Inc., Finding Nemo, and The Incredibles became massive commercial and critical successes, further solidifying Disney's position as a global entertainment powerhouse.

In 2009, Disney made another landmark acquisition with the purchase of Marvel Entertainment, which brought iconic comic book characters like Iron Man, Captain America, and Spider-Man under Disney's control. The acquisition of Marvel allowed Disney to enter the rapidly growing superhero film market, and it would soon lead to the creation of the Marvel Cinematic Universe (MCU), which became one of the most successful film franchises of all time.

In 2012, Disney made another pivotal acquisition, this time purchasing Lucasfilm, the company behind the Star Wars franchise. The purchase, which cost $4 billion, provided Disney with a beloved and expansive franchise that resonated with audiences across generations. The Star Wars franchise has been a major contributor to Disney's revenue, with new films, television series, theme park attractions, and merchandise all contributing to its success.

The Streaming Revolution: Disney+ and the Future

The rise of The Walt Disney Company took a major leap forward in 2019 with the launch of Disney+, Disney's own streaming platform. Disney+ allowed the company to compete directly with streaming giants like Netflix, Amazon Prime Video, and Hulu. The service was an immediate hit, thanks in large part to Disney's extensive content library, which includes classics like The Lion King and Aladdin, as well as new shows and movies from Pixar, Marvel, Star Wars, and National Geographic.

Disney+ rapidly attracted millions of subscribers, and the success of the platform has been a key driver of Disney's growth in recent years. In addition to Disney+, the company also owns ESPN+, a streaming service focused on sports, and Hulu, a platform that features television shows, movies, and original programming. Together, these platforms have given Disney a diverse and robust presence in the streaming space, further expanding the company's reach.

The company has also expanded its film and television offerings, producing major blockbuster films like Avengers: Endgame, Frozen II, and The Mandalorian. Disney's ability to produce high-quality, mass-appeal content has enabled it to remain a dominant force in the entertainment industry.

A Global Entertainment Empire

Today, The Walt Disney Company is one of the largest and most diversified media and entertainment conglomerates in the world. It operates in virtually every area of entertainment, including film production, television broadcasting, theme parks, retail, consumer products, and streaming services. The company owns and operates some of the most iconic and influential brands in the world, including Disney, Pixar, Marvel, Star Wars, and National Geographic.

Disney's ability to maintain its position as a leader in the entertainment industry is rooted in its commitment to creativity, innovation, and storytelling. The company has built an empire that spans the globe, with its films, television shows, merchandise, and theme parks reaching millions of people in virtually every country. Whether through animated classics, live-action blockbusters, or immersive theme park experiences, Disney continues to shape the entertainment world and captivate audiences around the world.

In conclusion, the rise of The Walt Disney Company is the story of an ambitious dream brought to life through sheer determination, creativity, and strategic thinking. Walt Disney's vision of creating a world where imagination could flourish has led to the creation of an empire that continues to entertain, inspire, and innovate. From humble beginnings in a small studio to becoming a global entertainment giant, Disney's rise reflects not just business success but the power of storytelling and creativity to shape the world.

The Expansion of Walt Disney's Legacy: Beyond Entertainment

As the Walt Disney Company continued its growth, it began to explore new avenues of expansion, breaking into different sectors that would further solidify its position as a global entertainment powerhouse. These ventures not only diversified Disney's offerings but also transformed it into a multifaceted conglomerate with influence in various aspects of the global economy. The expansion of its brand, from international markets to licensing and merchandise, would ultimately make Disney a ubiquitous presence around the world.

International Expansion: The Globalization of Disney

As early as the 1950s, Walt Disney's aspirations extended beyond the borders of the United States. Recognizing the universal appeal of its animation and theme parks, the company began its push into international markets. The first major milestone in this internationalization came in 1983 with the opening of Tokyo Disneyland. This marked the first Disney theme park outside of the United States, and its success was immediate, drawing millions of visitors from across Japan and the rest of Asia. The park's opening was significant not only for its cultural impact but also because it set the stage for future international Disney parks.

Over the years, Disney's international expansion continued, with the opening of Disneyland Paris in 1992, Hong Kong Disneyland in 2005, and Shanghai Disneyland in 2016. Each of these parks was tailored to meet the cultural preferences and unique market dynamics of their respective regions. For instance, Shanghai Disneyland incorporated elements of Chinese culture and mythology, making it a localized yet distinctly Disney experience. These global ventures have helped Disney cement its place as a leader in the global tourism and entertainment industries.

Beyond the theme parks, Disney also expanded its reach through international film distribution, broadcasting, and digital media platforms. The company's films and television shows are now broadcast worldwide, and Disney has localized its content to appeal to diverse audiences across Asia, Europe, the Middle East, and Latin America. The launch of Disney+ was an essential element of this strategy, as it allowed the company to penetrate global markets rapidly with its expansive library of films and television shows. With its international reach, Disney continues to serve as a bridge between cultures, helping to spread American entertainment across the globe while also incorporating diverse influences into its storytelling.

The Disney Brand: Licensing, Merchandise, and Consumer Products

Walt Disney's vision for his company was not limited to films and theme parks. He understood that the magic of Disney could be expanded into physical products, creating a vast consumer products empire that would generate substantial revenue. In the 1930s and 1940s, Disney began licensing Mickey Mouse and other popular characters for use on various merchandise items, including toys, clothing, and household products. This decision to market Disney characters through consumer goods was a groundbreaking move that laid the foundation for the company's merchandising success.

The company's first major licensing agreement came in 1930, when Disney allowed the character of Mickey Mouse to be used on a variety of products, from dolls to dishware. The merchandise quickly became a hit, and Mickey Mouse became the face of a growing consumer products industry that would encompass everything from apparel and toys to food products and home goods. Disney's merchandise operations would only grow with time, becoming one of the company's most profitable business segments.

Today, Disney's consumer products division is a multibillion-dollar industry, with licensed products being sold in every corner of the globe. The company's vast portfolio includes popular franchises such as Marvel, Star Wars, and Pixar, each contributing its own set of characters and storylines to the merchandise offerings. Disney-branded toys, clothing, books, and even food products are everywhere, making the company's characters a part of everyday life. For example, toys based on characters from the Pixar film Toy Story or the Marvel Cinematic Universe (MCU) continue to dominate the toy industry, generating millions in sales annually.

The Acquisition Strategy: Strengthening the Portfolio

Disney's strategy of acquiring other companies and intellectual properties has played a central role in the company's evolution. Through a series of high-profile acquisitions, Disney has been able to consolidate control over a vast array of popular franchises and brands. These acquisitions have allowed Disney to expand its reach into new genres, audiences, and platforms while simultaneously bolstering its creative capabilities.

The acquisition of Pixar Animation Studios in 2006 was a transformative moment for Disney. Pixar had already revolutionized animation with the release of Toy Story in 1995, the first feature-length film made entirely with computer-generated imagery (CGI). The studio continued to release groundbreaking films, such as Monsters, Inc., Finding Nemo, and The Incredibles, all of which were box office successes and critical darlings. Pixar's expertise in CGI animation was a perfect fit for Disney, which had traditionally relied on hand-drawn animation.

By acquiring Pixar for $7.4 billion, Disney gained control of one of the most successful animation studios in the world, allowing it to dominate the animation market for years to come. The merger allowed for a fusion of Disney's traditional animation prowess with Pixar's cutting-edge CGI technology, leading to the production of films like Up, Frozen, and Toy Story 3, which broke box office records and continued Disney's legacy of animated excellence.

The acquisition of Marvel Entertainment in 2009 for $4 billion brought another major set of assets into Disney's fold. Marvel's rich library of superhero characters, including Spider-Man, Iron Man, and Captain America, offered Disney access to an entire genre that was rapidly gaining popularity among audiences worldwide. The creation of the Marvel Cinematic Universe (MCU) revolutionized the superhero genre and made Disney a major player in the film industry. Films like The Avengers, Iron Man, and Guardians of the Galaxy became box-office juggernauts, and the MCU has since grown into one of the most lucrative and enduring franchises in cinematic history.

One of the most significant acquisitions in Disney's history was its purchase of Lucasfilm, the company behind the Star Wars franchise, in 2012. The $4 billion acquisition immediately gave Disney control over one of the most beloved and iconic franchises in the world. Star Wars had already garnered a massive fan base over several decades, and Disney's stewardship of the franchise brought about new films, television series, and an entire new wave of Star Wars-themed merchandise. The Star Wars saga, alongside the Marvel universe, has significantly contributed to Disney's continuing financial success and global presence.

The Digital Revolution: Embracing Technology and Innovation

In the 21st century, Disney began embracing new technologies to stay at the forefront of the entertainment industry. The launch of Disney+ in 2019 marked a pivotal moment in the company's transition to the digital age. The streaming service offered a comprehensive catalog of Disney's film and television content, from animated classics like The Lion King to new original programming like The Mandalorian, a Star Wars-themed series. Disney+ became an instant success, gaining millions of subscribers in its first year alone.

Beyond streaming, Disney has continued to integrate new technologies into its operations. The company has invested heavily in virtual reality (VR) and augmented reality (AR) experiences in its theme parks, allowing guests to engage with characters and environments in innovative new ways. The integration of cutting-edge animation technology, interactive media, and even artificial intelligence (AI) into Disney's creative processes has allowed the company to continue its tradition of storytelling and creativity well into the 21st century.

The Future of The Walt Disney Company: Innovation and Adaptation

As Disney continues to evolve, its future appears poised to be just as transformative as its past. With its deep roots in storytelling, technology, and creative innovation, the company is set to remain a leader in the entertainment industry for decades to come. The rise of digital platforms, the ongoing evolution of film production and distribution, and the integration of new technologies in entertainment are all areas where Disney is likely to continue expanding.

Disney's ability to adapt to changing consumer preferences, technological advancements, and market trends will be critical in ensuring its long-term success. The company's vast library of intellectual properties and its strong brand recognition provide a solid foundation for continued growth, whether through new content creation, acquisitions, or expanding its global footprint. As Walt Disney once said, "It's kind of fun to do the impossible," and this philosophy continues to guide The Walt Disney Company as it embarks on the next phase of its extraordinary journey.

(Current Status of Walt Disney Company)

The Walt Disney Company, often simply referred to as Disney, has evolved from a small animation studio into one of the largest and most diversified entertainment conglomerates in the world. As of today, Disney operates across multiple sectors, including film, television, theme parks, streaming services, and media networks. The company's global footprint and cultural influence continue to expand, driven by its commitment to innovation, creativity, and business expansion. However, it faces both challenges and opportunities as it navigates the ever-changing entertainment landscape.

A Diversified Entertainment Empire

Disney operates through various segments that contribute to its overall success. These segments include Media Networks, Parks, Experiences and Products, Studio Entertainment, and Direct-to-Consumer & International. Each of these business units plays a pivotal role in Disney's continued dominance of the entertainment industry.

1. Media Networks

Disney's Media Networks division remains one of the most critical parts of the company's revenue generation. The division includes cable networks like ESPN, ABC, Disney Channel, National Geographic, and Freeform, as well as television production and broadcasting operations. ESPN, in particular, has been a key driver of Disney's media business, despite facing challenges in the form of declining viewership of traditional cable TV and increased competition from streaming platforms.

The launch of Disney+ and the acquisition of other networks have further enhanced the company's dominance in the media space. Disney's broadcasting business also includes ABC, a prominent network that offers popular shows and news programming. In recent years, Disney has focused on expanding its presence in digital platforms and direct-to-consumer streaming services, moving away from traditional cable and satellite TV distribution models.

Additionally, Disney's acquisition of 21st Century Fox in 2019 brought valuable assets into its portfolio, including Fox's film and TV production, National Geographic, and regional sports networks. This move significantly bolstered Disney's position in the entertainment sector, adding more content to its already extensive library. The acquisition also marked a shift toward the importance of content ownership and vertical integration in the entertainment industry.

2. Parks, Experiences, and Products

The Parks, Experiences, and Products division is one of Disney's largest and most successful revenue-generating segments, encompassing its theme parks, resorts, cruise lines, and merchandise. Disney operates six resort locations globally: Walt Disney World in Florida, Disneyland in California, Disneyland Paris, Tokyo Disneyland, Hong Kong Disneyland, and Shanghai Disneyland. These parks are not just entertainment venues; they are immersive experiences that have become iconic symbols of Disney's brand.

Theme parks are a cornerstone of Disney's global business. In 2023, Walt Disney World and Disneyland, despite temporary setbacks during the COVID-19 pandemic, have seen consistent growth, attracting millions of visitors annually. The company continues to invest in upgrading and expanding its parks, with new attractions like Star Wars: Galaxy's Edge at Disneyland and Walt Disney World, the Avengers Campus, and several high-tech, immersive experiences that keep Disney's theme parks at the forefront of the industry.

Beyond theme parks, Disney also owns and operates a successful cruise line, Disney Cruise Line, which offers themed cruises that cater to families. These cruises are designed to provide guests with Disney experiences while they travel to various destinations, further enhancing the Disney brand's global reach.

Merchandise sales are another key aspect of the company's parks and products division. Disney's consumer products include toys, clothing, books, and various other items that feature characters and stories from Disney's movies, TV shows, and theme park attractions. The company has become one of the world's largest licensors of merchandise, with its products reaching children and families worldwide.

The pandemic impacted Disney's parks business significantly, as travel restrictions and social distancing measures forced the company to temporarily close its theme parks. However, Disney adapted quickly by enhancing its parks with new safety protocols and digital technology like mobile apps for reservations, ticketing, and virtual queues. Despite the setbacks, Disney's parks have remained a major contributor to the company's revenue, and as of 2023, the company has seen a strong rebound in attendance.

3. Studio Entertainment

Disney's Studio Entertainment division includes film production, including Disney-branded films, Pixar, Marvel Studios, Lucasfilm (home to the Star Wars franchise), and 20th Century Studios (formerly 20th Century Fox). The studio entertainment division is responsible for some of the most successful and influential films ever made, and it continues to drive much of Disney's global recognition.

The Marvel Cinematic Universe (MCU) has been a particularly important driver of Disney's studio entertainment business. With the acquisition of Marvel Entertainment in 2009, Disney gained control over a wealth of intellectual property, including iconic superhero franchises like Iron Man, Spider-Man, Captain America, and the Avengers. The MCU has become the highest-grossing film franchise in history, with movies like Avengers: Endgame and Avengers: Infinity War breaking box office records worldwide. The success of Marvel Studios has also led to the creation of television shows that tie into the MCU, further cementing Disney's dominance in the global entertainment industry.

The acquisition of Lucasfilm in 2012 brought Disney the globally beloved Star Wars franchise. Star Wars films, television shows, merchandise, and theme park attractions have made it a cornerstone of Disney's brand. In recent years, Disney has expanded the Star Wars universe with multiple films, the Disney+ series The Mandalorian, and new attractions at its theme parks, such as the Galaxy's Edge expansion.

Disney's acquisition of Pixar Animation Studios in 2006 also revolutionized the animated film industry. Pixar's films, such as Toy Story, Finding Nemo, The Incredibles, and Inside Out, have not only become cultural landmarks but also highly profitable ventures for Disney. The creative partnership between Disney and Pixar has led to numerous critically acclaimed animated films, which have helped to reinforce Disney's position as a leader in both animation and film production.

The Walt Disney Studios division also includes 20th Century Studios, the film studio behind major franchises such as Avatar and The Simpsons. Disney's acquisition of 20th Century Fox has allowed the company to diversify its content, adding new intellectual property to its portfolio. The success of James Cameron's Avatar: The Way of Water, released in December 2022, showed how Disney's investment in Fox's legacy properties continues to pay dividends.

Live-action films, such as The Lion King (2019), Aladdin (2019), and Beauty and the Beast (2017), have capitalized on nostalgia while appealing to new generations, continuing Disney's dominance in the film industry. The company has been successful in reimagining animated classics as live-action films, which often perform well at the box office and with audiences.

4. Direct-to-Consumer & International

Disney's direct-to-consumer segment, primarily centered around Disney+, has become one of the company's most essential growth areas. In 2019, Disney launched Disney+, a streaming service designed to compete with established giants like Netflix, Amazon Prime Video, and Hulu. Disney+ has seen rapid growth, attracting millions of subscribers worldwide with its vast content library, which includes Disney films, Pixar, Marvel, Star Wars, and National Geographic.

Disney+ has not only expanded the company's presence in the global streaming market, but it also allowed Disney to leverage its extensive back catalog of films and TV shows. The platform has become a central hub for Disney content, with original programming like The Mandalorian, WandaVision, Loki, and The Falcon and the Winter Soldier appealing to subscribers. Moreover, Disney has strategically aligned its direct-to-consumer content strategy with its existing franchises, creating synergy between its film, television, and streaming platforms.

The company's other streaming service, ESPN+, focuses on sports content and has become a significant player in the growing market for sports streaming. ESPN+ allows Disney to tap into the sports audience that has traditionally been loyal to cable TV. ESPN+ offers live sports programming, documentaries, and exclusive content that targets a different demographic compared to Disney+.

In addition to Disney+ and ESPN+, Disney owns Hulu, a streaming service that provides a mix of television, movies, and original programming. Hulu has been a strong performer in the U.S. market, offering content from Disney's vast library and third-party content providers. In 2023, Disney took full control of Hulu and began integrating the service more closely with its other streaming platforms.

Global Expansion and International Markets

Disney has made significant inroads into international markets, expanding its influence around the world. With theme parks in Paris, Hong Kong, Shanghai, and Tokyo, Disney has solidified its position as a global brand. The company continues to grow its international presence through its streaming platforms, with Disney+ now available in most major international markets.

The company's acquisition of 21st Century Fox helped it gain more access to international media markets, including a greater footprint in regions like India and Europe. Fox's television networks, such as Star India, have enabled Disney to compete more effectively in international broadcasting, particularly in the Asia-Pacific region.

Disney's commitment to global expansion extends beyond film and television. The company has also been investing in its theme park experiences around the world, with Shanghai Disneyland being one of its most successful international ventures. Disney has also focused on creating culturally relevant content for international markets, which has helped it build an even stronger fan base worldwide.

Disney facing challenges

While Disney remains an entertainment powerhouse, it is not without its challenges. The most notable of these is the shifting landscape of media consumption. With more consumers cutting the cord and moving away from traditional television, Disney faces increased pressure to continue growing its streaming platforms. The competition in the streaming space is fierce, and Disney+ must keep up with the quality and quantity of content offered by Netflix, Amazon, and other streaming services.

The company also faces growing scrutiny over its content strategy, particularly when it comes to balancing its various brands. Disney's legacy of family-friendly content must coexist with the darker, more mature content from its acquisitions, such as 20th Century Fox's films and Hulu's more adult-oriented programming. This balancing act has created some friction with audiences and critics, as Disney tries to manage its identity across multiple brands.

Another significant challenge for Disney has been the ongoing global economic uncertainty, particularly in light of inflation and the effects of the COVID-19 pandemic. The pandemic severely impacted Disney's theme park and cruise line businesses, which are traditionally key sources of revenue. Although the parks have rebounded, the company must adapt to changing consumer habits, including growing interest in digital experiences and reluctance to return to travel.

Finally, Disney's leadership and management team has been under some scrutiny. Bob Chapek, who succeeded Bob Iger as CEO in 2020, faced challenges managing the company through the pandemic and its subsequent recovery. However, in late 2022, Chapek was replaced by Bob Iger, who returned as CEO to help steer the company through the post-pandemic era and the evolving media landscape.

CHAPTER FIVE

Henry Ford – Ford Motor Company

(History of Henry Ford and Ford Motor Company)

The Early Years: Henry Ford's Background

Henry Ford, born on July 30, 1863, in Dearborn, Michigan, grew up in a family with modest means. His father, William, was a farmer, and his mother, Mary, ensured the family valued self-reliance and hard work—values that would define Ford's later business philosophy. From an early age, Ford exhibited a strong interest in machinery, developing a keen fascination with mechanical devices, engines, and watches. He spent hours tinkering and repairing, displaying his technical ingenuity. After completing his education in Dearborn, Ford moved to Detroit in 1879 to work as an apprentice machinist, setting the stage for his career in mechanical innovation.

Ford's early career involved working at several mechanical firms, including the Detroit Dry Dock Company and Thomas Edison's Electric Light Company. His time at Edison's company had a profound influence, sparking his interest in the possibilities of electric power and the nascent automotive industry. Ford's engineering skills culminated in 1896 with the creation of his first self-propelled vehicle, the "Quadricycle." While rudimentary, the Quadricycle was an important step in the development of the automobile and a sign of Ford's deep commitment to engineering and innovation.

Ford Motor Company: A New Beginning

Ford founded the Ford Motor Company in 1903 with a bold mission: to produce affordable, reliable automobiles for the average American. The early years were marked by financial struggles and fierce competition from established manufacturers. However, Ford's unwavering belief in mass production and standardized techniques would soon change the industry forever.

In 1908, Ford introduced the Model T, an affordable car designed for the working class. Priced at $850, it was significantly cheaper than most cars on the market at the time. The Model T's real breakthrough wasn't just in its design but in the manufacturing processes Ford employed. Rather than relying on skilled artisans to produce each car individually, Ford implemented mass production techniques that drastically reduced production costs. This would lay the groundwork for the assembly line revolution in manufacturing.

The Assembly Line: Revolutionizing Manufacturing

Ford's most revolutionary contribution to the world of manufacturing was the introduction of the moving assembly line in 1913 at the Highland Park plant in Michigan. This innovation dramatically altered the way goods were produced. By allowing parts to move along a conveyor belt while workers remained in fixed positions, Ford reduced the time it took to assemble a Model T from more than 12 hours to just 93 minutes. The efficiency of this system cut production costs, which allowed Ford to lower the price of the Model T even further, making it accessible to a broader population.

The impact of the assembly line was felt far beyond the Ford Motor Company. Industries across the globe adopted similar techniques, transforming manufacturing processes in various sectors and making mass production a hallmark of modern industry. This shift not only revolutionized car manufacturing but also had a lasting impact on economic growth and industrial practices throughout the 20th century.

The $5 Workday: A Bold Move in Labor Relations

In 1914, Ford introduced the $5 workday—double the prevailing wage in many American factories at the time. The $5 wage had a profound impact on the lives of his workers, allowing them to better support their families and significantly reducing turnover. Ford saw the $5 workday as not only a moral obligation but a strategic business move. He believed that by paying workers more, they would be able to afford the very cars they were building, expanding the customer base for Ford vehicles.

The $5 workday sparked national attention, and while critics initially saw it as a risky decision, it soon proved successful. Workers were more loyal, productivity improved, and the Ford Motor Company became a model for fair labor practices in industrial America. Ford's commitment to improving worker welfare marked a turning point in the labor movement, setting a new standard for wages in the industrial workplace.

Expansion and Global Reach

By 1918, Ford's Model T had become a household name, and the Ford Motor Company had become a dominant force in the automobile industry. In that year, half of all cars on American roads were Model Ts. As demand grew, Ford expanded the company's operations internationally, setting up plants in Canada, England, and other parts of Europe. This global expansion solidified Ford's position as a leader in the automotive world.

Ford did not limit himself to just cars. His company ventured into other sectors, including tractor manufacturing and even airplanes. This diversification helped Ford Motor Company remain resilient, even as the automobile industry faced new challenges in the years ahead. In 1927, Ford introduced the Model A, responding to changing consumer preferences with updated technology and a more modern design. The Model A's success reaffirmed Ford's ability to adapt to the evolving market.

The Great Depression and Resilience

The onset of the Great Depression in the 1930s presented unprecedented challenges. Car sales plummeted, financial difficulties mounted, and labor unrest reached a peak. However, Ford's commitment to innovation, even in the face of adversity, ensured the company's survival. The introduction of the Ford V8 engine in 1932 became one of the company's most successful products, helping Ford maintain its competitive edge during this difficult period.

Despite public controversies, particularly related to labor strikes, Ford continued to push for improvements in working conditions. The violent 1937 labor strike at the River Rouge plant, known as the "Battle of the Overpass," was a dark chapter in Ford's legacy. However, Ford's resolve to improve labor relations and modernize his operations allowed the company to eventually weather the economic storm.

World War II: Contributing to the War Effort

During World War II, Ford Motor Company shifted its focus from consumer vehicles to war materials. Ford's Willow Run plant became famous for producing one B-24 bomber every 55 minutes—an impressive feat that showcased the company's ability to scale its operations for wartime production. Ford's contributions to the war effort not only helped secure the Allied victory but also demonstrated the power of mass production in times of national need.

Ford's ability to adapt its manufacturing capabilities for wartime production highlighted the company's strategic approach and reinforced its importance as an industrial powerhouse. Ford Motor Company played a pivotal role in the war effort, producing essential materials and boosting American industrial capacity.

Postwar America: Innovation and Legacy

The end of World War II marked the beginning of a new era for Ford Motor Company. In the 1950s, Ford introduced iconic models such as the Ford Thunderbird and the Ford Mustang. The Mustang, in particular, became a symbol of American automotive culture, known for its style, speed, and performance. Ford's innovation during this period helped solidify its dominance in the postwar automotive market.

In the 1960s and 1970s, Ford further expanded its global presence and became a leader in automotive safety and environmental concerns. The company played a key role in developing safety features like seatbelts and continued to introduce new models that appealed to a growing consumer base.

The Modern Era: Challenges and Technological Advancements

In the 1980s and 1990s, Ford faced increasing competition from foreign manufacturers, particularly Japanese automakers. In response, the company began restructuring its operations to improve quality control and reduce costs. Ford also made significant investments in new technologies, including electric vehicles and autonomous driving.

By the early 21st century, Ford embraced a new wave of innovation. The introduction of the Ford Mustang Mach-E, an all-electric vehicle, and the development of self-driving technology demonstrated the company's commitment to sustainability and future-ready solutions. In addition to producing environmentally-friendly vehicles, Ford continued to explore new green manufacturing practices and energy-efficient technologies, keeping pace with the evolving demands of the automotive market.

Ford's Enduring Legacy

Henry Ford passed away on April 7, 1947, but his impact on the automotive industry and the global economy continues to resonate today. Ford's innovations in mass production, his progressive approach to labor relations, and his visionary leadership reshaped manufacturing and set new standards for industry. The Ford Motor Company, now one of the largest and most influential automakers in the world, continues to lead the way in innovation, efficiency, and sustainability.

Ford's legacy lives on in every vehicle produced, and his commitment to making cars affordable, improving working conditions, and driving technological advancement remains an integral part of the company's philosophy. Today, Ford continues to evolve, adapting to the challenges of the modern world, but its roots in Ford's vision of innovation and accessibility remain firmly planted.

"If you think you can do a thing or think you can't do a thing, you're right."- Henry Ford

sulting in long production times and high costs.

Ford's solution was to introduce a moving assembly line, in which each car would be moved along a conveyor belt, with workers performing a specific task at each stage of production. This new system dramatically reduced the time it took to assemble a car. The time to build a car dropped from over 12 hours to just 93 minutes. This innovation allowed Ford to produce cars at a much faster rate, significantly reducing the cost of production and making the Model T even more affordable.

(Rise of Ford Motor Company)

The Rise of Henry Ford and the Ford Motor Company

The story of Henry Ford and the Ford Motor Company is not only a tale of personal triumph but also a narrative of profound social and industrial transformation. The rise of Ford, a figure once considered just another ambitious inventor, to the creator of a global automotive empire, is a journey marked by innovation, risk-taking, and an unyielding commitment to progress. This section will explore the origins of Henry Ford, the founding of the Ford Motor Company, the development of groundbreaking manufacturing techniques, and the way Ford's vision fundamentally changed the American economy and labor practices. It will detail how Ford's leadership, values, and innovations helped propel both himself and his company to extraordinary heights, leaving an enduring legacy in the automotive world and beyond.

Henry Ford: From Farm Boy to Inventor

Born on July 30, 1863, in Dearborn, Michigan, Henry Ford came from humble beginnings. He was the son of William Ford, a farmer, and Mary Ford, who had emigrated from Ireland. Growing up on the family farm, Ford was not particularly fond of farming itself. Instead, he found himself drawn to the workings of machines and engines. This early passion for mechanics would define his career and his impact on the world. Ford's intellectual curiosity and inventive spirit began to take shape during his youth. In his spare time, he would take apart and repair watches and engines, developing an intricate understanding of how machinery functioned.

At the age of 16, Ford left the farm and moved to Detroit to pursue his interest in mechanics. He worked as an apprentice machinist and later with the Detroit Dry Dock Company. Ford's experiences in these early jobs provided him with the skills and knowledge that would eventually allow him to design and build his own automobile. In 1891, Ford began working for the Edison Illuminating Company, where he quickly rose through the ranks to become an engineer. It was here that he met Thomas Edison, who would become one of his key mentors.

Edison's influence on Ford was significant. Ford admired Edison's ability to innovate and bring new ideas to life, which inspired him to pursue his own dream of creating a self-propelled vehicle. In 1896, after years of experimentation, Ford completed his first car, the "Quadricycle." This vehicle, a simple frame with four bicycle wheels and a gasoline-powered engine, was crude by modern standards, but it represented the beginning of what would become a groundbreaking journey in the automotive industry.

The Birth of Ford Motor Company

In 1901, after a few unsuccessful attempts to form a car company, Ford struck out on his own with financial backing from a group of Detroit investors, including John and Horace Dodge. The Ford Motor Company was officially founded in 1903. However, the company struggled in its early years, facing financial difficulties and stiff competition from established manufacturers like the Cadillac and Oldsmobile. Ford's early attempts to build a reliable, affordable car were met with skepticism and failure, but he was undeterred.

Ford was determined to produce a car that would be affordable and accessible to the average American. In 1908, after years of trial and error, Ford introduced the Model T, a revolutionary car that would change the automotive industry forever. The Model T was designed with simplicity and durability in mind. It was easy to operate, repair, and maintain, and it was affordable for the average person. Unlike previous cars, which were expensive and available only to the wealthy, the Model T was priced at $850, making it accessible to millions of Americans.

The Model T became an instant success. By 1914, Ford had sold over 250,000 units, and the Model T was on its way to becoming one of the best-selling cars in history. Ford's ability to produce a car that was both affordable and reliable was a testament to his ingenuity and foresight. But Ford wasn't content to rest on his laurels—he was determined to change the way cars were made, making them even more affordable and accessible.

First Factory Of ford motors

Revolutionizing Manufacturing: The Assembly Line

In 1913, Henry Ford introduced the moving assembly line at the Highland Park plant in Detroit, a decision that would revolutionize the manufacturing industry. Ford's assembly line was the culmination of years of experimentation with ways to streamline production. Before the assembly line, each car was built by hand, with workers performing individual tasks on each car. This method was time-consuming and inefficient, re

The moving assembly line also had a profound impact on the labor market. By breaking down the production process into smaller, specialized tasks, Ford was able to increase productivity and reduce the number of workers needed on each car. This allowed Ford to offer higher wages and better working conditions to his employees. In 1914, Ford introduced the $5 workday, doubling the average wage for factory workers at the time. This bold move not only attracted skilled workers to Ford's factories but also helped to reduce turnover and increase productivity.

The introduction of the assembly line also had far-reaching implications for the wider industrial landscape. Ford's assembly line became a model for other manufacturers, not just in the automotive industry, but in virtually every sector of manufacturing. Mass production, as a result, became a cornerstone of industrial practice in the 20th century, shaping the modern economy and workforce.

Inside view of the Ford's Manufacturing Unit

Ford's solution was to introduce a moving assembly line, in which each car would be moved along a conveyor belt, with workers performing a specific task at each stage of production. This new system dramatically reduced the time it took to assemble a car. The time to build a car dropped from over 12 hours to just 93 minutes. This innovation allowed Ford to produce cars at a much faster rate, significantly reducing the cost of production and making the Model T even more affordable.

Expanding the Ford Motor Company

Ford's success with the Model T and the assembly line marked a turning point in both his career and the history of the automobile. The Ford Motor Company was now a global enterprise, and Ford was an industry leader. As Ford's success grew, so did his company's reach. By 1918, half of all cars on American roads were Model Ts. The Ford Motor Company expanded internationally, opening plants in Canada, England, and Europe. Ford also ventured into producing tractors and airplanes, further diversifying his business interests.

Ford's decision to expand internationally was crucial in establishing the Ford Motor Company as a global powerhouse. By opening plants in other countries, Ford was able to tap into new markets and increase production, further cementing his company's place as a leader in the automotive industry. This global reach was essential in solidifying the company's position as an industry giant and was a key factor in Ford's ability to weather the economic downturns of the 1920s and 1930s.

The Model A and the Great Depression

The 1920s were a period of rapid change in the automotive industry. Consumer preferences were shifting, and Ford's dominance in the market was beginning to wane. In response, Ford introduced the Model A in 1927, a new car that was designed to appeal to a broader audience. The Model A was a success, but the economic downturn that followed the stock market crash of 1929 and the onset of the Great Depression posed significant challenges for the company.

During the Great Depression, the Ford Motor Company faced a drastic decline in sales and mounting financial difficulties. Unemployment rates were soaring, and consumer spending was at an all-time low. Despite these challenges, Ford remained committed to his vision. He continued to focus on innovation, producing the V8 engine in 1932, which became one of the most popular engines in automotive history. Although Ford faced criticism for his handling of labor relations during the

Depression, he remained resolute in his commitment to the principles of mass production and efficiency.

Ford's ability to adapt to the economic challenges of the Great Depression was a testament to his resilience and foresight. The introduction of the V8 engine and continued investment in new technologies helped to position the Ford Motor Company for recovery as the economy began to rebound in the 1940s.

World War II: A Shift in Focus

The outbreak of World War II in 1939 marked another turning point in Ford's history. The war effort required massive production of military vehicles, aircraft, and weapons. Ford shifted its focus from producing civilian automobiles to manufacturing war materials. The Willow Run plant, a sprawling factory located outside of Detroit, became a symbol of American industrial might. During the war, the Willow Run plant produced one B-24 bomber every 55 minutes, a feat that demonstrated Ford's ability to adapt to large-scale production demands.

Ford's contribution to the war effort was critical in securing the Allied victory. The company's production capabilities and innovative manufacturing techniques helped supply the military with the materials needed to fight the war. This period of wartime production further cemented Ford's reputation as a leader in industrial manufacturing.

Postwar America: The Mustang and the Legacy

After the war, Ford turned its attention back to consumer automobiles. The 1950s and 1960s were a period of economic prosperity in America, and Ford was quick to capitalize on the growing demand for automobiles. In 1964, Ford introduced the Ford Mustang, a car that would become an icon of American performance and style. The Mustang was an instant success, and its popularity helped to solidify Ford's position as a dominant force in the automotive industry.

The postwar period also saw Ford's continued commitment to innovation. In the 1960s and 1970s, Ford focused on safety, environmental concerns, and fuel efficiency. The company played a significant role in the development of seatbelt safety standards and introduced new models that were more fuel-efficient, responding to the oil crises of the 1970s.

Ford's leadership and vision throughout the 20th century left an indelible mark on both the automotive industry and American society. The company's commitment to mass production, efficiency, and innovation revolutionized not only the automobile industry but also manufacturing as a whole. Ford's ability to adapt to changing economic and technological landscapes ensured that the Ford Motor Company remained at the forefront of the automotive world, even as new competitors emerged.

(Current Status of Ford Motor Company)

Ford's Market Position and Financial Performance

Ford Motor Company remains one of the largest and most influential automakers globally, with a presence in over 100 markets. Despite intense competition from major players like General Motors, Toyota, Volkswagen, and new electric vehicle manufacturers, Ford maintains a strong position, especially in its home market, the United States. In 2023, Ford was the second-largest U.S.-based automaker by total vehicle sales, following General Motors and outpacing Stellantis, which owns Chrysler.

In recent years, Ford has demonstrated resilience and adaptability in the face of significant challenges, including the COVID-19 pandemic, global supply chain disruptions, and the semiconductor chip shortage. Ford's 2022 financial performance was a testament to this, as the company posted $158 billion in revenue and a net income of $1.3 billion, reflecting a solid recovery from the pandemic-induced downturn. The company's ability to pivot rapidly to meet demand for high-margin trucks and SUVs has played a crucial role in this recovery.

The Ford F-Series, particularly the F-150, has long been a cornerstone of the company's success, with the F-150 holding a dominant share of the U.S. full-size pickup market. In recent years, Ford has diversified its lineup by expanding its SUV and truck offerings. Models such as the Ford Maverick, a compact hybrid pickup, and the Ford Bronco, which was reintroduced to target off-road enthusiasts, have helped Ford grow its market share while catering to evolving consumer preferences.

In 2023, Ford also launched its commercial vehicle division under the Ford Pro brand, which includes electric vehicles like the E-Transit van. This strategic move underscores Ford's commitment to supporting businesses transitioning to electric fleets, tapping into an emerging segment that is vital for the future of EV adoption.

Transition to Electric Vehicles (EVs)

A pivotal focus for Ford's future lies in its transition to electric vehicles (EVs), driven by the global shift toward sustainability and stricter environmental regulations. In response, Ford has committed substantial investments, amounting to billions of dollars, to electrify its vehicle lineup.

The company's push into EVs began with the launch of the Ford Mustang Mach-E SUV in late 2020. The Mach-E was well-received for its design, range, and performance, positioning it as a competitor to Tesla's Model Y. As part of a broader strategy to electrify its lineup, Ford also introduced the F-150 Lightning, an all-electric version of its iconic F-Series truck. The F-150 Lightning, which debuted in 2021, has gained attention for combining the durability and power of the F-Series with the energy efficiency and sustainability of electric technology. It has been praised for its towing capacity, quick acceleration, and lower operating costs compared to traditional gasoline-powered models.

In addition to its passenger vehicles, Ford has expanded its EV portfolio to include commercial vehicles such as the E-Transit van, aimed at businesses seeking to electrify their fleets. This effort is part of a broader initiative that includes the formation of the Ford Pro division, which offers fleet customers electric vehicles, charging infrastructure, and other related services.

Ford has pledged to invest $22 billion in electrification and advanced technologies through 2025, with plans to launch at least 40 new electric models globally. This initiative is aligned with the company's broader goal of achieving carbon neutrality by 2050 and reducing CO_2 emissions from its vehicles by 40% by 2035.

A critical element of Ford's EV strategy is its partnership with SK Innovation, aimed at building battery plants in North America. This move supports the company's efforts to reduce reliance on external suppliers for battery materials, ensuring a more secure and cost-effective supply chain as it ramps up EV production.

Challenges in the Automotive Industry

The automotive industry is grappling with several challenges, many of which have impacted Ford's operations. The COVID-19 pandemic, global supply chain disruptions, and the ongoing semiconductor shortage have all hindered Ford's ability to meet demand for its vehicles, particularly high-demand models like the F-150. These issues have resulted in production delays and inventory shortages.

Despite these setbacks, Ford has proactively addressed supply chain challenges by diversifying its supplier base, adopting flexible manufacturing systems, and leveraging real-time digital technologies to monitor and manage its supply chains more effectively.

Ford also faces increasing competition from newer players in the EV market, including Tesla, Rivian, and Lucid Motors. These companies have established themselves as key competitors in the electric vehicle space, forcing Ford to innovate rapidly. Ford has responded by intensifying investments in software development, autonomous driving technology, and EVs, while continuing to refine its traditional vehicle offerings.

Ford's Autonomous Driving and Mobility Solutions

Ford is also positioning itself at the forefront of autonomous driving technology. The company has made significant investments in this area, partnering with startups like Argo AI to develop fully autonomous vehicles. Through its Ford Smart Mobility division, Ford is exploring new transportation solutions, including car-sharing, ride-hailing, and autonomous delivery services.

In 2021, Ford and Argo AI announced plans to launch autonomous ride-hailing services in Miami and Austin, Texas, in collaboration with Lyft. This initiative will feature Ford Escape hybrids equipped with Argo AI's self-driving technology, allowing Ford to test the feasibility of autonomous vehicles in urban environments.

Ford is also developing autonomous delivery solutions, collaborating with Walmart and Postmates to create self-driving delivery vehicles. These vehicles aim to revolutionize logistics by reducing costs and increasing efficiency in the delivery sector.

Sustainability and Environmental Responsibility

Sustainability is a key focus for Ford as the company works to reduce its environmental impact. Beyond its transition to electric vehicles, Ford is taking steps to minimize the carbon footprint of its manufacturing processes. The company has committed to achieving carbon neutrality globally by 2050, with an intermediate goal of reducing CO_2 emissions from its vehicles by 40% by 2035.

Ford has also made strides in sustainability within its vehicle design. For instance, the F-150 Lightning is made using recycled aluminum, and the company is incorporating sustainable materials, such as soy-based foam, in vehicle interiors. These initiatives reflect Ford's dedication to both sustainability and efficiency in its product offerings.

Ford's Brand and Consumer Relations

Ford has maintained a strong and reliable brand, built on a legacy of performance, innovation, and quality. Iconic models like the F-Series trucks, the Mustang, and the Bronco continue to attract loyal customers. Ford's commitment to providing a diverse range of vehicles—spanning from performance cars to family SUVs—has allowed it to appeal to a broad consumer base.

In addition to its vehicles, Ford is embracing digital technologies to enhance customer experiences. The FordPass app, for example, enables customers to remotely access their vehicles, check their vehicle's health, and schedule service appointments. By focusing on connected vehicle technologies and 5G-enabled systems, Ford is positioning itself as a leader in the evolving automotive landscape.

Ford's Role in the Global Supply Chain

Ford's global supply chain is vast, and managing it efficiently is critical to the company's success. The company sources materials and parts from around the world, with manufacturing facilities in more than 50 locations across six continents. While disruptions such as the semiconductor shortage have affected production, Ford has taken steps to mitigate risks by diversifying suppliers and adopting AI technologies to predict and address supply chain disruptions.

Sustainability is also a priority within Ford's supply chain. The company is working closely with suppliers to reduce carbon emissions and incorporate eco-friendly materials. As part of its broader sustainability goals, Ford is aiming to make its production facilities carbon-neutral by 2035, a commitment that extends to its supply chain.

Ford and Artificial Intelligence: Advancing Technology

Ford is at the cutting edge of AI innovation, integrating artificial intelligence into several aspects of its operations. AI plays a key role in the development of autonomous driving technology, with Ford working closely with Argo AI to create self-driving vehicles. These cars use AI algorithms to analyze data from sensors and cameras, allowing them to make real-time decisions on the road.

Ford also leverages AI in manufacturing, using AI-powered robots to enhance production efficiency, improve quality control, and predict maintenance needs. Furthermore, AI is being integrated into customer service, with tools like AI chatbots and virtual assistants improving customer interactions and satisfaction.

In terms of safety, Ford has integrated AI into its advanced driver-assistance systems (ADAS), including features like adaptive cruise control, lane-keeping assist, and automatic emergency braking, which enhance vehicle safety and driver experience.

Ford's Strategic Partnerships and Collaborations

To accelerate innovation and stay competitive in the rapidly evolving automotive industry, Ford has formed several strategic partnerships. One of the most notable is its collaboration with Google, which focuses on using cloud computing and AI to enhance Ford's connected vehicle services, manufacturing operations, and customer experiences.

Ford also partners with Volkswagen to jointly develop electric and autonomous vehicles, sharing development costs and leveraging each other's expertise. Additionally, Ford has joined forces with various charging infrastructure providers to expand the availability of EV charging stations, helping ensure that customers have access to reliable, fast-charging solutions.

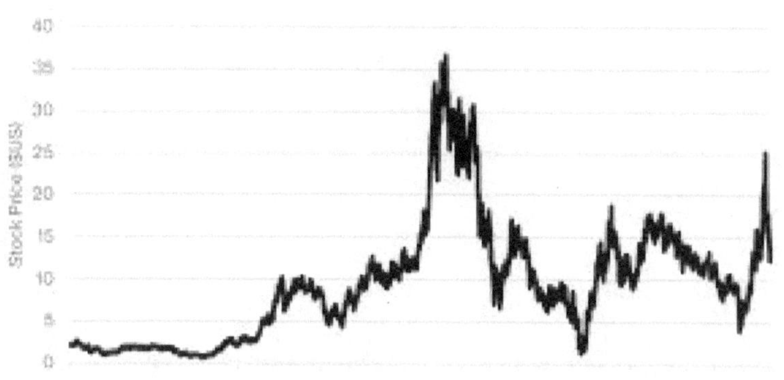

"Ford Motors Stock Growth Over the Years"

Part II: The Tech Revolutionaries

As we transition into Part II of our exploration, we delve into the heart of the Tech Revolutionaries era, a phase defined by innovation, disruption, and the rise of transformative technologies that have reshaped industries, economies, and societies at large. In this section, we will focus on the key figures and companies that drove the technological advances of the 21st century, shaping the digital age as we know it today.

Part II will highlight the individuals and organizations that not only mastered new technologies but also pioneered their use in ways that revolutionized the world. These innovators—often referred to as the Tech Revolutionaries—include visionary entrepreneurs, engineers, and business leaders who saw the potential in emerging fields such as computing, artificial intelligence, cloud computing, and biotechnology. Their contributions have led to profound changes in how we live, work, and interact with the world around us.

We will cover notable figures like Steve Jobs and Bill Gates, who built the foundational platforms for personal computing; Elon Musk, whose ventures in electric vehicles, space exploration, and renewable energy have redefined industries; and Jeff Bezos, who created Amazon, transforming global commerce and the way people shop. The work of pioneers like Mark Zuckerberg, who revolutionized social media, and Larry Page and Sergey Brin, who reshaped the way we access information with Google, will also be integral to our discussion.

In addition to individual stories, we will explore the companies that emerged from their visions and how these companies have pushed the boundaries of technological possibilities. We will discuss the rise of Silicon Valley as the epicenter of global innovation, and how startups, venture capital, and a culture of risk-taking have all contributed to the rapid acceleration of technological advancement.

We will also examine the profound societal impacts these tech revolutionaries have had, from the democratization of information to the disruption of traditional business models. The challenges and controversies faced by these leaders—ranging from ethical dilemmas and privacy concerns to regulatory scrutiny—will be explored in depth. This section aims to provide an understanding of the powerful forces driving the tech landscape, offering insights into the future trajectory of innovation and its potential to transform our world.

CHAPTER SIX

STEVE JOBS – APPLE INC.

(History of Steve Jobs and Apple Inc)

Steve Jobs, born on February 24, 1955, in San Francisco, California, was a visionary entrepreneur, inventor, and innovator whose work revolutionized the world of personal computing and consumer electronics. He is most famously known for co-founding Apple Inc. and bringing to life products like the iPhone, iPad, iPod, and the Macintosh, which collectively transformed how we interact with technology. Steve Jobs' influence on design, business, and technology is unparalleled, making him one of the most significant figures in modern history. His journey, however, was not one of unbroken success. It was a story of passion, setbacks, persistence, and transformation, all of which are essential to understanding the impact he made.

Jobs was adopted by Clara and Paul Jobs, a working-class couple in Mountain View, California. His biological parents, Joanne Schieble and Abdulfattah Jandali, were both graduate students when they had Steve, but they were unable to raise him and decided to place him for adoption. Although his biological parents later reunited and married, Jobs would have little connection with them and would be raised by the Jobs family.

His adoptive father, Paul, worked as a machinist, and his mother, Clara, was an accountant. Growing up in the heart of Silicon Valley, the young Jobs was immersed in a culture of innovation and technology. His father taught him the art of craftsmanship, which sparked his lifelong passion for design and perfection.

Steve Jobs showed early signs of brilliance and curiosity, particularly in the fields of electronics and engineering. By the time he reached high school, Jobs had formed a strong friendship with Steve Wozniak, a brilliant electronics engineer. Wozniak had an affinity for computers and was often tinkering with electronic projects, and it was through him that Jobs became captivated by the possibilities of computers. Their shared interests, along with Jobs' business acumen, would lay the foundation for the creation of Apple. Their bond grew stronger as they began collaborating on projects, each contributing their unique talents—Wozniak's technical expertise and Jobs' vision and sense of design.

After high school, Jobs attended Reed College in Portland, Oregon. However, he dropped out after just one semester, a decision that puzzled many, but which he later justified by saying it allowed him to pursue his interests with greater freedom. Even though he was no longer formally enrolled, Jobs continued to audit classes, especially a calligraphy course that would have a lasting impact on his design philosophy. Jobs often referred to this class as a turning point in his life, saying that it helped him appreciate the importance of typography and aesthetics in product design. Little did anyone know that the lessons he learned in this class would shape the future of Apple's products, particularly when it came to the company's focus on simplicity, beauty, and functionality.

In 1976, Steve Jobs, alongside Wozniak and Ronald Wayne, co-founded Apple Computer Inc. in Jobs' parents' garage. With their combined expertise, they developed the Apple I, one of the first personal computers to be sold as a fully assembled kit. Although the Apple I was relatively basic compared to later computers, it was the beginning of a groundbreaking journey in personal computing. The Apple I's commercial success was modest, but it provided the foundation for what would come next: the Apple II.

The Apple II, introduced in 1977, was the first truly successful product from Apple. It was a fully assembled personal computer that featured color graphics, a design that was revolutionary at the time. The Apple II marked a breakthrough in personal computing, not just because of its advanced technical specifications, but also because of its accessibility. It was easy to use and came with a wide range of software. By the early 1980s, the Apple II had captured the imagination of consumers and businesses alike. Its success laid the groundwork for Apple's future expansion and helped establish the company as a leader in the rapidly growing personal computer market.

Despite the success of the Apple II, Jobs and Apple were not immune to challenges. In the early 1980s, the company faced difficulties with its next major product, the Apple III. The Apple III was intended to be a follow-up to the Apple II, but it was plagued by design flaws, reliability issues, and high production costs. The failure of the Apple III, combined with the pressure to continue innovating, set the stage for Jobs' next ambitious project: the Lisa. The Lisa was a pioneering computer, one of the first to feature a graphical user interface (GUI). Although the Lisa was a technical marvel, its $10,000 price tag made it inaccessible to most consumers. It was eventually discontinued due to poor sales.

Despite the setback with the Lisa, Jobs' vision for a computer with a graphical user interface continued to evolve. In 1984, Apple released the Macintosh, which would go on to become one of the most iconic products in tech history. The Macintosh was the first commercially successful computer to feature a graphical user interface, which made it far more intuitive and user-friendly than other personal computers at the time. It was marketed with the famous "1984" Super Bowl ad, directed by Ridley Scott, which cast Apple as a liberator in the battle against the conformity of

"Big Brother"-like corporations.

However, despite the hype and innovative features, the Macintosh was not an immediate commercial success. Sales were slow, partly due to its high price and the limited availability of compatible software. Apple's internal struggles also intensified, especially between Jobs and other executives, including CEO John Sculley. Tensions reached a breaking point in 1985, when Jobs was ousted from Apple. The man who had co-founded the company was forced to leave, marking one of the most dramatic moments in Silicon Valley's history.

Rather than retreating, Jobs set out on a new path. In 1985, he founded NeXT, a computer company that aimed to create high-end workstations for universities and businesses. NeXT computers were technologically advanced, featuring cutting-edge hardware and the NeXTSTEP operating system, which would later influence Apple's own operating systems. However, NeXT was never financially successful, as its products were too expensive for most businesses to adopt. Despite the company's lack of widespread commercial success, NeXT's innovations would eventually play a crucial role in Apple's revival when Jobs returned to the company in 1997.

Around the same time, Jobs also acquired The Graphics Group from George Lucas, which would eventually be renamed Pixar. Pixar's journey into the world of animation would change the industry forever. With Jobs' leadership, Pixar transitioned from a computer graphics company into a powerhouse of animated filmmaking. The release of Toy Story in 1995, the world's first feature-length computer-animated film, catapulted Pixar to international fame. The success of Toy Story helped establish Pixar as a leader in animation, and in 2006, Disney purchased Pixar for $7.4 billion, making Jobs Disney's largest shareholder.

Meanwhile, Apple was struggling. By the late 1990s, the company was facing severe financial difficulties, with market share slipping and its product lineup growing stale. In 1997, as Apple teetered on the brink of bankruptcy, the company bought

NeXT for $429 million, bringing Jobs back to the company. Jobs took control of Apple's direction and immediately set out to revitalize the company. He streamlined Apple's product offerings, focusing on a few key products that could be executed flawlessly. He also simplified the company's complex product line and shifted the company's focus toward design and ease of use.

One of Jobs' first successes was the introduction of the iMac in 1998. Designed by Jonathan Ive, the iMac was a bold, colorful, and innovative take on the personal computer. It featured a translucent plastic shell and a compact design that was far more visually appealing than the clunky beige boxes that dominated the market at the time. The iMac was a huge hit, and its success marked the beginning of Apple's comeback.

Jobs continued to expand Apple's influence, launching the iPod in 2001. The iPod revolutionized the music industry, making digital music portable and accessible. In 2003, Jobs also launched the iTunes Store, which allowed users to legally purchase and download music online. The success of the iPod and iTunes helped Apple establish itself as a dominant force in consumer electronics.

In 2007, Apple introduced the iPhone, which would go on to change the entire tech industry. The iPhone combined the functionality of a phone, an iPod, and an internet device in a sleek, touch-screen package. The iPhone's success was unprecedented, and it helped usher in the smartphone revolution. It was the first smartphone to truly integrate the internet, touch-screen navigation, and a variety of apps in a seamless user experience.

The iPhone also marked the beginning of Apple's focus on creating an integrated ecosystem of products and services. Apple continued to release groundbreaking products like the iPad, Apple Watch, and Apple TV, each of which helped to establish the company's place at the forefront of consumer technology.

Jobs' leadership at Apple was not just about technology; it was about creating a brand that resonated deeply with consumers. Apple became synonymous with quality, design, and innovation, and Jobs was its figurehead, the embodiment of the company's values. He built a company that wasn't just about making money—it was about changing the world. Jobs was a perfectionist who pushed his teams to create the best possible products. He was known for his demanding and sometimes abrasive leadership style, but his ability to inspire those around him was undeniable. He built Apple into one of the most valuable and influential companies in the world, with a cult-like following of loyal customers.

Steve Jobs' impact on the world is immeasurable. His work transformed the technology industry and changed the way we live, work, and communicate. Through Apple, NeXT, and Pixar, Jobs created products and services that revolutionized computing, entertainment, and consumer electronics. His passion for design, innovation, and simplicity set a new standard for what products could be. Jobs' insistence on creating products that were not just functional but beautiful and intuitive set Apple apart from its competitors and made it one of the most iconic brands in history.

Steve Jobs died on October 5, 2011, after a long battle with pancreatic cancer. His death was met with an outpouring of tributes from people around the world who had been inspired by his work. Jobs' legacy lives on in the products that Apple continues to create and in the companies that were inspired by his approach to business and innovation. He left behind a world that was profoundly changed by his ideas, vision, and determination. Today, Apple remains one of the most successful and influential companies in the world, and Steve Jobs' spirit continues to inspire countless entrepreneurs, designers, and engineers.

"Your time is limited, so don't waste it living someone else's life." -Steve Jobs

(Rise of Steve Jobs and Apple.INC)

The rise of Steve Jobs and the evolution of Apple Inc. is one of the most compelling stories of innovation, disruption, and success in the history of technology. From humble beginnings in the Silicon Valley garage to creating a global empire, Jobs' vision and relentless pursuit of perfection revolutionized not just technology, but entire industries. To truly understand the depth and magnitude of his impact, we need to explore the various phases of his career, his philosophy, the trials he faced, and the eventual triumphs that reshaped the world.

The Genesis of a Visionary

Steve Jobs' story begins in the 1950s, long before he became the face of Apple Inc. Born on February 24, 1955, in San Francisco, California, Jobs was adopted by Paul and Clara Jobs. Raised in the heart of the Bay Area, Jobs was exposed to the emerging technology scene in Silicon Valley, where engineers and innovators were beginning to push the boundaries of what was possible with computers. His early years were marked by a rebellious streak, a trait that would define his future endeavors.

Jobs was an inquisitive child, constantly experimenting with electronics and mechanical gadgets. His adoptive father, Paul Jobs, was a machinist, and his mother, Clara Jobs, was an accountant. Together, they fostered an environment where Steve could explore and develop his interests. While still in high school, Jobs was already intrigued by electronics, spending his afternoons tinkering with devices. It was during this time that he met Steve Wozniak, a brilliant engineer who would later become his co-founder at Apple.

Jobs attended Homestead High School in Cupertino, California, where he formed a close friendship with Wozniak. Wozniak, who was several years older than Jobs, was a brilliant engineer with a deep understanding of electronics. The two bonded over their shared interest in technology, and Wozniak soon began mentoring Jobs in the technical aspects of electronics. This friendship would later prove pivotal in the creation of Apple.

After graduating from high school in 1972, Jobs enrolled at Reed College in Portland, Oregon. However, his college journey was short-lived. Jobs dropped out after just one semester, realizing that the traditional education system wasn't a good fit for him. Instead, he chose to audit classes that piqued his interest, including a calligraphy class that would later have a profound influence on the design philosophy he would apply at Apple. Jobs' decision to drop out of college is often cited as a key moment in his life, as it allowed him to pursue a nontraditional path and hone his skills in ways that wouldn't have been possible in a conventional educational setting.

The Birth of Apple: A Visionary Collaboration

In 1976, the seeds of Apple were planted in Jobs' parents' garage. Along with Wozniak and Ronald Wayne, a third co-founder, Jobs set out to create a computer that would be accessible to everyone, not just tech enthusiasts and engineers. Wozniak was the technical genius behind the Apple I, while Jobs focused on the vision, design, and marketing of the product. The Apple I was one of the first personal computers to be sold as a complete package, and it marked the beginning of Jobs' journey as an entrepreneur.

The Apple I was a simple, functional machine, but it laid the foundation for what would become a revolutionary company. The trio's hard work and determination paid off, and they were able to sell enough units to keep their fledgling company afloat. Jobs understood the potential of personal computers, but he also recognized that the key to making them widely accepted was to make them more user-friendly and accessible. This idea became central to the development of Apple's future products.

In 1977, Apple introduced the Apple II, a machine that would prove to be a game-changer. Unlike the Apple I, which required users to assemble the machine themselves, the Apple II was a complete system with a color display, a keyboard, and integrated software. This made it much easier to use for the average consumer. The Apple II's success was a turning point for Apple, and it propelled the company into the mainstream. The demand for the Apple II was so high that Apple had to scale its operations rapidly, marking the first of many significant growth phases for the company.

The Macintosh Revolution: Breaking New Ground

Despite the success of the Apple II, Jobs had a vision for the future of computing that went far beyond what was possible with the existing technology. He wanted to create a computer that was intuitive, user-friendly, and visually appealing—a machine that would democratize computing for everyone, not just tech enthusiasts. This vision led to the creation of the Macintosh.

In the early 1980s, Jobs gathered a team of engineers and designers to develop the Macintosh, a computer that would challenge the dominance of IBM and other companies in the personal computing market. The Macintosh would be the first personal computer to feature a graphical user interface (GUI), which allowed users to interact with the machine through icons, windows, and a mouse rather than the traditional command-line interface.

The Macintosh was launched in 1984, and it was immediately heralded as a groundbreaking product. The famous "1984" television commercial, directed by Ridley Scott, portrayed the Macintosh as the savior that would free the world from the oppressive rule of IBM. The commercial, which aired during the Super Bowl, became iconic, and it set the tone for Apple's marketing campaigns in the years to come.

Despite the Macintosh's technological innovations, it struggled in the marketplace. Its high price, limited software availability, and relatively poor performance compared to IBM-compatible PCs led to slow sales. The Macintosh's commercial failure created significant tension within Apple, and this tension would eventually lead to a power struggle between Jobs and CEO John Sculley, who had been hired by Jobs himself.

The Fall and Rise of Jobs: A Second Act

In 1985, after a series of internal conflicts and power struggles, Steve Jobs was forced out of Apple, the company he had founded. It was a painful and humbling experience for Jobs, who had poured so much of his energy and passion into the company. But rather than retreating, Jobs took this setback as an opportunity to reinvent himself.

After leaving Apple, Jobs founded NeXT, a computer company that aimed to create high-end workstations for universities and businesses. NeXT's computers were beautiful, powerful, and technologically advanced, but their high price tags made them unaffordable for most. The company struggled financially, but it helped Jobs refine his vision for what a computer could be. NeXTSTEP, the operating system developed by NeXT, would later play a pivotal role in the development of Apple's software after Jobs returned to the company.

During this time, Jobs also purchased a small animation company called Pixar. Pixar, which was originally focused on producing computer graphics hardware, would eventually become a leading force in the animation industry. Under Jobs' leadership, Pixar developed groundbreaking films like Toy Story, A Bug's Life, and Monsters, Inc. These films revolutionized the animation industry and proved that computer-generated imagery (CGI) could be used to create compelling, emotionally resonant stories.

In 2006, Disney acquired Pixar for $7.4 billion, and Jobs became the largest individual shareholder of Disney. This acquisition marked the beginning of Jobs' influence on the entertainment industry, in addition to his role in shaping the technology sector.

The Return to Apple: A New Era of Innovation

In 1997, Apple was in crisis. The company was on the brink of bankruptcy, and its products had fallen behind the competition. Apple's once-vibrant brand had become associated with stagnation, and the company was in desperate need of direction. This was when Steve Jobs made his dramatic return to the company he had founded.

Jobs' return to Apple marked the beginning of a new era for the company. He immediately set about streamlining the company's operations, focusing on a smaller range of products, and refocusing Apple's design philosophy. One of the first major successes under Jobs' leadership was the iMac, a sleek, colorful, all-in-one computer that stood in stark contrast to the beige, boxy designs that were typical of computers at the time.

The iMac was a commercial success, and it helped to restore confidence in Apple. Jobs' design philosophy, which emphasized simplicity, elegance, and user experience, was beginning to take root. Apple's products were no longer just functional; they were beautiful, intuitive, and emotionally engaging.

The iPod and the Digital Music Revolution

In 2001, Apple introduced the iPod, a portable digital music player that would change the way people listened to music. The iPod was an instant success, offering a sleek design, a large storage capacity, and ease of use. It was the first device that truly made digital music mainstream, and it laid the foundation for Apple's dominance in the consumer electronics market.

The iPod's success was amplified by the launch of the iTunes Store in 2003, which allowed users to purchase and download music legally. The iTunes Store revolutionized the music industry, providing a legitimate alternative to piracy while making it easier for consumers to access music on demand.

Together, the iPod and iTunes created a digital ecosystem that transformed the way people consumed music. Jobs' vision for a seamless, integrated experience was coming to fruition, and Apple's brand was becoming synonymous with innovation and quality.

The iPhone: A Revolution in Mobile Technology

In 2007, Apple introduced the iPhone, a device that would revolutionize the mobile phone industry. The iPhone combined a phone, a music player, and a computer all in one device, and it featured a revolutionary touch-screen interface that replaced physical buttons. The iPhone's sleek design, intuitive interface, and seamless integration with iTunes made it an instant success.

The iPhone did not just change the phone industry—it changed the entire landscape of consumer electronics. Jobs' vision for a device that could combine all aspects of digital life into one seamless package had come to fruition. The iPhone was a mobile computer that allowed users to make phone calls, browse the internet, listen to music, watch videos, and run applications—all on a single device.

The iPhone was a game-changer in terms of both hardware and software. It introduced the concept of an app store, where third-party developers could create applications that expanded the functionality of the device. This created an entirely new industry—the mobile app economy—which has since grown into a multi-billion dollar industry.

The iPad and Beyond: Shaping the Future

Following the success of the iPhone, Apple continued to innovate with the introduction of the iPad in 2010. The iPad was a tablet computer that bridged the gap between smartphones and laptops. It was lightweight, portable, and offered a large, touch-sensitive screen that was perfect for browsing the web, reading books, and consuming media.

The iPad became another blockbuster product for Apple, further solidifying Jobs' reputation as one of the greatest innovators of all time. Jobs' philosophy of creating products that were not only functional but also beautiful and user-friendly had become the cornerstone of Apple's success.

Apple continued to push the boundaries of innovation under Jobs' leadership, launching new products like the Apple Watch, AirPods, and various iterations of the iPhone and iPad. Each new product was an evolution of Jobs' original vision for a seamless, integrated digital experience.

Jobs' Legacy and Impact on the World

Steve Jobs passed away on October 5, 2011, after a long battle with pancreatic cancer. His death marked the end of an era, but his influence continues to be felt in the technology industry and beyond. Jobs' legacy is defined by his vision for the future, his commitment to excellence, and his ability to inspire others to think differently.

Jobs' impact on the world extends far beyond the products he created. He changed the way we think about design, business, and technology. Through Apple, Jobs showed that technology could be both functional and beautiful, and that it could improve the lives of millions of people around the world.

Today, Apple remains one of the most valuable companies in the world, and its products continue to shape the way we live, work, and interact with technology. Jobs' philosophy of innovation, simplicity, and user experience is still embedded in the DNA of Apple, and it serves as a model for companies around the world.

Steve Jobs was more than just a businessman; he was a visionary who understood the power of technology to change the world. His story is a testament to the importance of following one's passion, challenging the status quo, and never settling for mediocrity. His legacy will continue to inspire generations of innovators and entrepreneurs to come.

(Current Status of Apple.INC)

Apple Inc.: The Pinnacle of Technological Innovation and Growth

Apple Inc. stands as one of the most successful companies in history, a beacon of innovation, resilience, and market dominance. It has established itself not just as a technology company, but as a cultural and economic phenomenon that has shaped the way people interact with technology and perceive brands. From the original vision of Steve Jobs and Steve Wozniak to today's massive global enterprise, Apple has continuously redefined technological standards and created a powerful ecosystem that brings together hardware, software, and services.

As of 2024, Apple holds an irreplaceable position in the global market, with a market capitalization that surpasses $3 trillion, making it the most valuable company in the world. The company's ability to innovate year after year has been key to maintaining this dominance, expanding into diverse product lines, and building an unmatched ecosystem of services. But this success didn't come overnight. It was built through decades of navigating industry challenges, pioneering groundbreaking technology, overcoming crises, and adapting to changing market conditions. Apple's story is not just one of products, but of vision, culture, leadership, and relentless pursuit of excellence.

Apple's Current Market Position

Apple's market performance has remained unparalleled in several respects, especially in terms of profitability and innovation. As of 2024, Apple is consistently ranked as one of the largest and most influential tech giants in the world. Apple's brand is synonymous with luxury, innovation, and quality, which has allowed it to command premium prices for its products and services. Apple's financials consistently reflect strong sales, resilient earnings, and a robust balance sheet, all of which showcase the power of its brand.

Market Capitalization and Revenue Growth

In the fiscal year 2023, Apple reported annual revenues exceeding $390 billion and a net income of over $100 billion. Apple's market capitalization has surged to over $3 trillion, marking it as not only the most valuable tech company but also the first company to hit this monumental valuation. It has established a unique position where it does not rely solely on a singular product, but on a well-rounded ecosystem of products, services, and future projects that continue to drive sustained growth.

Revenue Breakdown

Apple's revenue model is incredibly diverse, with significant contributions from hardware, services, and wearables. Although hardware sales, particularly iPhones, are still the dominant driver of Apple's financial performance, the company's services business has experienced exceptional growth. In fact, services now contribute more than 20% of Apple's total revenue. This shift marks Apple's strategy to reduce its dependency on hardware sales, an important step in ensuring stability and longevity in an increasingly saturated market.

Services such as iCloud, Apple Music, Apple TV+, Apple Arcade, and the App Store have expanded their footprint. The App Store alone continues to generate billions of dollars annually, with over 500 million active users globally. Apple Music, while competing with Spotify, Amazon Music, and others, has carved a significant niche in the music streaming industry. Its competitive edge comes from exclusive content, integration with Apple's ecosystem, and the high quality of its music library.

While hardware remains the cornerstone of Apple's revenue streams, services are expected to play an increasingly important role in the company's financial future. Apple's strategic focus on recurring revenue through subscriptions and services aims to create a more predictable income flow and allow the company to weather fluctuations in hardware sales.

Apple's Product Portfolio: A Market Leader in Innovation

Apple's product portfolio is expansive, but each product line shares common threads: elegance, simplicity, and functionality. Apple is known for its meticulous attention to design and its ability to seamlessly integrate hardware and software. This integrated approach has allowed Apple to deliver an unmatched user experience, one that is fluid, reliable, and intuitive. Let's take a closer look at some of the key categories within Apple's portfolio.

1. The iPhone: A Legacy of Innovation

The iPhone remains Apple's flagship product, the keystone of its product ecosystem, and the device that made Apple synonymous with smartphones. Launched in 2007, the iPhone revolutionized the telecommunications industry and has consistently set the standard for mobile phones worldwide. Apple's iPhone line-up has seen various iterations, each one improving on the last. The iPhone 15, launched in 2023, showcased Apple's commitment to performance and design, featuring the A17 Bionic chip, an advanced camera system, and new design elements like the Dynamic Island interface. These upgrades were aimed not just at maintaining competitive edge but at further enhancing the user experience with every generation.

The iPhone remains the dominant player in the smartphone market, contributing the largest share to Apple's annual revenue. Despite a saturated global smartphone market, Apple's strategy of premium pricing, combined with frequent product upgrades and an incredibly loyal customer base, has allowed it to maintain substantial profits and continue leading the market.

The iPhone's impact goes beyond just its technical specifications. The iPhone revolutionized how people interact with technology—ushering in the era of mobile apps, touch interfaces, and constant connectivity. It's not just a phone, but a lifestyle device that allows users to connect with others, consume media, shop, play games, manage their finances, and monitor their health—all from a single device.

2. Mac: The Premium Computing Experience

Apple's line of Mac computers—MacBook Air, MacBook Pro, iMac, and Mac Studio—has played a major role in the company's success. These computers continue to represent the gold standard for personal computing, used by professionals, creatives, students, and enterprises alike.

With the release of the M1 chip in 2020, Apple signaled a new era for the Mac. The transition from Intel processors to Apple's custom-designed chips was a bold move that paid off handsomely. The M1 and later M2 chips are highly regarded for their efficiency and processing power, delivering a computing experience that is fast, responsive, and energy-efficient.

Apple's focus on design and integration has allowed the Mac to stand out in a crowded market. The sleek, minimalist designs, powerful internal components, and integration with macOS make it a popular choice for creative professionals and everyday users. The macOS operating system, with its intuitive interface and rich features, creates a seamless experience for users who are already entrenched in Apple's ecosystem.

The MacBook Air and MacBook Pro models have become the go-to devices for professionals and students, balancing performance and portability. Meanwhile, the iMac continues to be an iconic desktop solution, known for its stunning Retina displays, exceptional audio, and powerful computing capabilities.

3. iPad: Reinventing the Tablet Category

The iPad, Apple's tablet offering, continues to lead the tablet market with consistent innovation. Since its debut in 2010, the iPad has undergone significant evolution, adapting to both consumer needs and enterprise demands. Today, the iPad Pro, iPad Air, and iPad mini serve a broad range of consumers, from casual users and students to professional artists and creative workers.

The iPad Pro, in particular, has become a serious tool for professionals, competing with laptops and desktops in terms of productivity. The inclusion of Apple's M1 and M2 chips has transformed the iPad Pro into a device capable of handling complex tasks such as video editing, 3D rendering, and software development. Paired with accessories like the Apple Pencil and Magic Keyboard, the iPad Pro has gained a strong following among digital artists, designers, and professionals looking for a portable yet powerful device.

The iPad's ability to function as both a tablet and a laptop replacement, combined with its extensive app ecosystem, has made it one of the most versatile devices in Apple's portfolio. The iPad continues to be central to Apple's vision of computing as an experience that blends entertainment, productivity, and creativity.

4. Wearables: Apple Watch and AirPods

Apple has made a significant push into wearables, with products like the Apple Watch and AirPods playing crucial roles in its expanding product ecosystem. The Apple Watch has become the best-selling smartwatch globally, thanks to its combination of health monitoring features, fitness tracking, and deep integration with the iPhone.

In 2024, the Apple Watch Series 9 continues to offer groundbreaking health features, including heart rate monitoring, ECG, blood oxygen levels, sleep tracking, and new fitness features that integrate with the broader Apple ecosystem. The WatchOS software ensures that users get the best possible experience, from managing their health data to controlling music and messages, all from their wrist.

AirPods, too, have become an essential product for iPhone users. Known for their superior sound quality, noise-canceling capabilities, and seamless connection to Apple devices, AirPods have become a ubiquitous accessory for users on the go. The new AirPods Pro models with Active Noise Cancellation and spatial audio continue to enhance the user experience, making AirPods a core part of Apple's wearables division.

5. Services: A Growing Sector

While Apple's hardware continues to define its legacy, its services segment has evolved into a major growth driver. With offerings like the App Store, iCloud, Apple Music, Apple TV+, Apple News+, Apple Arcade, and more, Apple is positioning itself as not just a hardware company, but a digital services powerhouse. In fact, services now account for a growing portion of Apple's revenue.

The App Store remains one of the most important digital platforms in the world, providing a venue for developers to reach millions of customers globally. The revenue generated from apps, subscriptions, and in-app purchases continues to fuel Apple's growth in this segment. Apple has also been aggressively expanding its cloud storage services, with iCloud being an essential component of the Apple ecosystem for backing up user data and syncing across devices.

Apple Music competes directly with other streaming services like Spotify and Amazon Music, but it has carved a niche through exclusive content, integration with the Apple ecosystem, and superior audio quality. The addition of Apple TV+ added another layer to Apple's entertainment offerings, featuring original TV shows and movies that have garnered critical acclaim and recognition.

Apple has also ventured into gaming with Apple Arcade, a subscription service that offers users access to premium games without ads or in-app purchases. While not as large as its competitors like Xbox Game Pass or PlayStation Now, Apple

Arcade still represents a growing segment within the services portfolio.

Apple Stock Performance, 2000-2016

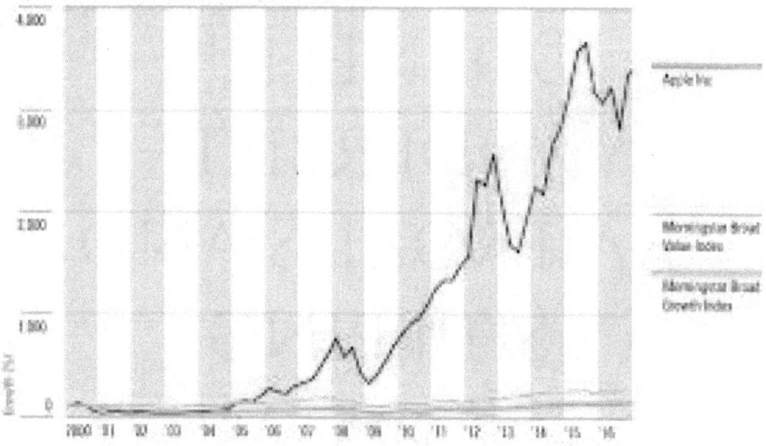

CORNELIUS VANDERBILT – RAILROADS AND SHIPPING

(History of Cornelius Vanderbilt – Railroads and Shipping)

The Early Life of Cornelius Vanderbilt and the Origins of His Companies

Early Life and Family Background

Cornelius Vanderbilt, born on May 27, 1794, in Staten Island, New York, grew up in circumstances far removed from the luxurious lifestyle associated with his later years. Vanderbilt would go on to become one of the wealthiest men in American history, but his early life was marked by hardship, resourcefulness, and a relentless drive to escape poverty. He was born into a modest household, the fourth of nine children born to Cornelius Vanderbilt Sr. and Phebe Hand. His father was a farmer and a small-time boatman, and his mother, though descended from a wealthier family, was far from living a life of comfort.

Vanderbilt's father, Cornelius Sr., was a hardworking yet financially struggling individual. Their household, located on the waterfront of Staten Island, was in constant financial turmoil, with the family often relying on the meager earnings from his father's modest business ventures to make ends meet. As a child, Vanderbilt had a firsthand understanding of the weight of financial struggle, and he became acutely aware of the daily challenges that his parents faced. While his father worked as a farmer, managing a small plot of land that yielded only modest returns, the family's true livelihood was dependent on the income from boat transport and ferry services—a small but crucial business that the family ran along the waterways surrounding Staten Island.

Though Cornelius Sr. struggled, his work as a farmer and boatman exposed the young Cornelius to the world of trade and transportation. These formative years in a working-class environment profoundly shaped his understanding of commerce, resourcefulness, and the critical role of transportation in commerce. Young Cornelius was already familiar with the infrastructure of canals, ships, ferries, and waterways, even though his family's business was not particularly prosperous. Despite the lack of wealth, there was a constant lesson in the practicalities of running a small enterprise—lessons that Vanderbilt would later expand upon in his own business ventures.

Phebe Hand, Cornelius's mother, was from a family that had once enjoyed more wealth. However, the Hand family's fortune had dissipated by the time Phebe married Cornelius Sr. Although Phebe's family did not possess the significant wealth that might have made them part of the social elite, her connections and previous social status would later provide young Vanderbilt with some important networking opportunities. Phebe's background offered the young Cornelius an understanding of the importance of social ties, and this, combined with his father's work ethic, helped shape his overall character.

At the heart of Vanderbilt's early life was the tension between his familial circumstances and his desire to rise above them. His parents' financial difficulties, combined with his own early exposure to the dynamics of business and trade, instilled in him a sense of determination that would remain with him throughout his life. He was acutely aware of his family's struggles, and in many ways, they motivated him to push harder toward his own entrepreneurial success.

Education and the Lack of Formal Schooling

Though Vanderbilt came from a family with little financial stability, he was not without intellectual influences. However, the difficulties of his family's finances led to the curtailment of his formal education. The education that young Cornelius received was minimal by the standards of his time, and he attended school only briefly. At the age of 11, his formal schooling ended, as the financial strain of the family required him to begin working to support them. His early life therefore reflects the harsh reality of many working-class families of the time, where children often had to leave school to contribute to the family income.

Vanderbilt's limited education did not, however, impede his ability to learn and grow in other ways. His most valuable lessons came not from textbooks, but from his direct involvement in the family's boat and ferry business. As a teenager, he quickly became immersed in the operations of ferrying people and goods across the waterways of Staten Island and Manhattan. Here, he learned the basic principles of logistics, transportation, and commerce, as well as the nuances of managing a small business.

Even though his formal education was brief, the lessons he learned from his father's boat business proved crucial in shaping his entrepreneurial drive. Vanderbilt's aptitude for business was apparent early on. It was his involvement in the ferry service, where he learned the importance of punctuality, reliability, and efficiency, that would lay the foundation for his future ventures. As a result of this early exposure to the world of transportation,

Vanderbilt developed a deep understanding of the business, along with the practical knowledge needed to navigate the complexities of running a ferry service.

The Development of an Entrepreneurial Spirit

The drive to improve his circumstances was woven into the fabric of Cornelius Vanderbilt's character from a young age. Although his family's business was small and underfunded, young Cornelius already exhibited an entrepreneurial spirit. He began taking on more responsibilities within the business and developed a keen sense of how to increase profits. As a teenager, he learned about the costs of maintenance, the logistics of scheduling, and the financial management of a small service-oriented business. Vanderbilt's hunger for success and financial independence drove him to seek ways to make his operations more efficient and profitable.

As an entrepreneur-in-training, he made strategic decisions early on that would influence his future path. For example, even at the age of 16, Vanderbilt made his first major business move by borrowing $100 from his mother to purchase a small boat. This purchase marked the beginning of his steamboat empire. By operating his own ferry between Staten Island and Manhattan, Vanderbilt gained invaluable experience in business management, customer service, and competition. He also realized early on that providing a reliable service at competitive rates would help him establish a loyal customer base, which would serve him well as he grew his business.

Vanderbilt's entry into the ferry business was a pivotal moment in his career. Unlike many others who might have seen a small ferry service as a limited venture, he saw it as a stepping stone to greater opportunities. His initial success in ferry operations revealed his keen ability to identify gaps in the market and capitalize on them. As he continued to expand his ferry routes, he began to develop a reputation for being a savvy and hardworking businessman.

The Steamboat Revolution

By the 1820s, steam-powered vessels had begun to revolutionize transportation, especially on rivers and waterways. The advent of the steamboat was a transformative development for the United States, as it provided a means to travel both upstream and downstream with ease. While the basic concept of steam power had been around for some time, it was in the early 19th century that the technology truly came into its own. Vanderbilt, recognizing the potential of this new technology, decided to expand his business from ferries to steamboats.

The steamboat was a significant leap forward in transportation. It allowed for faster, more reliable service on long-distance river routes, and it was not restricted by wind or currents like traditional sailboats. By embracing the steam-powered vessel, Vanderbilt set himself apart from his competitors, many of whom still relied on slower, less reliable sailboats. In 1829, Vanderbilt purchased his first steamboat, the Perseverance, a large and powerful vessel that enabled him to expand his operations beyond the New York harbor.

Vanderbilt's move into the steamboat industry was a bold decision that would forever change the course of his career. By focusing on steamboat transportation, he was able to offer a more efficient service, which in turn allowed him to undercut his competitors on price while still delivering a superior experience to customers. His fleet of steamships grew rapidly as demand for faster, more reliable transportation grew.

Rivalries and Legal Battles: Gibbons v. Ogden

As Vanderbilt's business expanded, he inevitably encountered competition, and one of the most significant challenges he faced came from Thomas Gibbons, a wealthy businessman who had been granted a monopoly by the state of New York to operate steamships between New York and New Jersey. Gibbons, through his legal battles and aggressive tactics, sought to keep Vanderbilt from entering certain lucrative markets.

One of the key legal battles in this rivalry was the case Gibbons v. Ogden (1824), which centered on the issue of interstate commerce and the rights of states versus the federal government. In this case, Gibbons, who held a federal license to operate steamships, challenged the New York monopoly granted to Ogden. The case was ultimately decided in favor of Gibbons, with the U.S. Supreme Court ruling that interstate commerce was under the jurisdiction of the federal government, thus invalidating state-granted monopolies.

This ruling was a significant victory for Vanderbilt. It opened up new opportunities for his business, allowing him to expand his steamship operations into new territories without interference from state-imposed monopolies. Vanderbilt understood the implications of this ruling, and he wasted no time in capitalizing on the new legal landscape. He was now free to expand his steamboat empire across state lines, a decision that would prove critical in his continued rise to prominence.

The California Gold Rush and Expansion

As Vanderbilt's steamship business flourished, he began looking to new opportunities for expansion. One of the most significant events that would shape his business in the 1840s was the California Gold Rush. The Gold Rush attracted thousands of miners, adventurers, and settlers heading west to California in search of fortune. Vanderbilt, seeing an opportunity to provide efficient transportation to California, seized upon the demand for fast travel and established a steamship route between New York and California via the Isthmus of Panama.

This route was one of the first direct steamship services between the East Coast and California, and it became immensely popular. Vanderbilt's ability to identify the needs of his customers and meet them with speed and efficiency helped to solidify his reputation as one of the preeminent businessmen of his time. By leveraging his steamship fleet, he was able to generate significant profits, and his wealth and influence continued to grow.

The Foundations of a Legacy

By the time Vanderbilt reached middle age, his business empire had grown far beyond the small ferry service he had started with. His early ventures into the steamboat business, his rivalry with Gibbons, and his expansion into the lucrative California Gold Rush trade set the stage for his future success in the railroad industry. Cornelius Vanderbilt's early life and the foundations of his business empire were shaped by a combination of innate business acumen, relentless drive, and a keen ability to spot and seize opportunities. His transition from ferryboats to steamboats, and later to railroads, exemplified his forward-thinking approach to business—one that would eventually make him one of the wealthiest and most influential men in American history.

(Rise of Railroads and Shipping)

The Rise of Cornelius Vanderbilt and His Railroad Empire
The Shift from Steamships to Railroads: A Strategic Move
By the mid-1850s, Cornelius Vanderbilt had already earned considerable wealth and influence through his steamship ventures. But as the country's industrial landscape rapidly transformed, Vanderbilt began to see that the railroad industry could offer even greater opportunities. Railroads could connect the industrial centers of the Northeastern U.S. to the Midwest and beyond, transporting goods and people across vast distances more efficiently than steamships could over land.

Vanderbilt recognized the shift in transportation needs and pivoted his focus from ships to trains. His first major foray into railroads came in 1863 with the acquisition of the New York and Harlem Railroad. Although small and struggling at the time, Vanderbilt's business acumen allowed him to revive it by introducing more effective management and cost-cutting strategies.

Aggressive Expansion and Consolidation

After taking control of the New York and Harlem Railroad, Vanderbilt quickly set his sights on other railroads to expand his empire. His goal was simple: consolidate the railroads under a single banner to create an efficient and widespread transportation network. Through a series of strategic acquisitions—including the Hudson River Railroad and the Lake Shore and Michigan Southern Railway—Vanderbilt began to build an interconnected system of rail lines stretching from New York City to Chicago, Boston, and beyond.

One of the most significant moments in Vanderbilt's rise occurred in 1869 when he successfully gained control of the New York Central Railroad. This acquisition solidified his status as the dominant player in the railroad industry. By 1870, the New York Central and Hudson River Railroad was one of the largest and most profitable railroads in the U.S. It became the backbone of his growing empire and a critical piece of American infrastructure.

Vanderbilt was known for his aggressive and sometimes ruthless tactics. His vast fortune allowed him to outmaneuver competitors, often buying them out or forcing mergers. He was less concerned with building the companies from the ground up than with consolidating them into a unified system that would give him full control of transportation in the region.

Technological Advancements and Infrastructure Innovation

Vanderbilt's genius wasn't limited to acquisitions. He understood that a railroad's success depended on more than just control of the land and lines—it needed to be efficient, innovative, and reliable. He was among the first railroad magnates to invest heavily in modernizing the infrastructure.

He replaced the old iron tracks with newer, stronger steel tracks, which were more durable and capable of supporting heavier loads. This change improved the safety and capacity of his railroads, allowing them to run faster and carry more freight. In addition to upgrading the tracks, Vanderbilt also invested in new locomotives and passenger cars, ensuring that his trains could travel reliably and quickly.

One of his most significant infrastructure investments was in the development of double-track lines. These allowed trains to operate more frequently and reduced delays, boosting the overall efficiency of the system. Vanderbilt also focused on enhancing operational management to streamline train schedules, reducing bottlenecks and improving profitability.

The New York Central Railroad: Symbol of Success

By the time Vanderbilt passed away in **1877**, his New York Central Railroad had become one of the most advanced and profitable railroads in the country. It was a symbol of modern railroading, with its steel tracks, cutting-edge locomotives, and reliable service. Vanderbilt had built a railroad network that connected key cities and played a central role in the American economy.

Under his leadership, the New York Central became a critical link between major industrial centers and helped facilitate the movement of raw materials, finished goods, and people. The efficiency of the system played a major part in accelerating industrial growth, particularly in the northeastern United States.

The Ruthless Tactics of a Business Mogul

Vanderbilt was both respected and reviled for his business practices. On one hand, his ability to consolidate railroads, streamline operations, and build a vast network of rail lines was a remarkable feat. On the other hand, his aggressive tactics—such as using his immense wealth to outbid competitors and force mergers—earned him a reputation as a monopolist.

His no-holds-barred approach to business was a defining feature of his legacy. Critics often accused him of being ruthless, particularly in his dealings with smaller railroad owners whom he crushed or forced into submission. He frequently employed underhanded methods to gain control, such as undermining competitors through price wars or political manipulation. His willingness to use financial power to ensure dominance in the market was a hallmark of his strategy.

Despite these tactics, Vanderbilt's ability to shape the American transportation landscape cannot be overstated. He built a network that fueled the growth of the American economy, providing the necessary infrastructure to move goods and people across the nation.

Philanthropy and Vanderbilt's Lasting Legacy

Vanderbilt's fortune continued to grow throughout his life, making him one of the wealthiest individuals in the world by the time of his death. Yet, despite his financial success and monopolistic methods, Vanderbilt left behind a complex legacy.

In addition to his business accomplishments, he also made significant contributions to education. In 1873, he donated $1 million to establish Vanderbilt University in Nashville, Tennessee. This generous donation was one of the largest philanthropic contributions of its time and has had a lasting impact on American education.

Vanderbilt's contributions to education, along with his work in transportation, cemented his place in history. His vision for the future of America—rooted in technological innovation and a robust, interconnected transportation system—was ahead of its time. His railroads helped knit the country together, enabling economic growth and accelerating industrialization.

Vanderbilt's legacy is felt even today, as his work laid the foundation for modern transportation and urbanization. Though his methods were often criticized, his impact on the American economy, infrastructure, and education is undeniable. Today, the railroads he built continue to serve as critical arteries for the nation's freight and passenger transportation.

In sum, Vanderbilt's rise was marked by his ability to recognize new opportunities, his ruthless business strategies, his investments in technological innovation, and his enduring legacy as a philanthropist. Through his railroads, he not only transformed transportation but helped propel America into the modern industrial age. His life remains a testament to ambition, vision, and the power of strategic expansion in shaping the course of history.

"Life should not be a journey to the grave with the intention of arriving safely in a pretty and well preserved body, but rather to skid in broadside in a cloud of smoke"-Cornelius Vanderbilt

(Current Condition of Vanderbilt's Railroad Empire)

Current Condition of Vanderbilt's Railroad Empire

The Legacy of Cornelius Vanderbilt

Cornelius Vanderbilt, a prominent industrialist and philanthropist, played an essential role in shaping the landscape of American transportation during the 19th century. His empire—largely centered around railroads—was one of the most influential in the nation's history. Vanderbilt's vision led to the creation of the New York Central Railroad (NYC), a system that became the backbone of the American industrial revolution and propelled the United States into the modern era. But his legacy didn't end with his death in 1877; rather, it set the stage for a series of corporate transformations and mergers that would extend far beyond his passing.

Today, the remnants of Vanderbilt's railroad empire continue to influence the structure and function of American transportation. What was once a highly competitive landscape of various railroad lines, under the control of a few key industrialists, has evolved into a complex web of companies that now form the heart of the American freight system. These entities not only operate within the parameters established by Vanderbilt but also continue to shape new technological innovations, environmental policies, and economic considerations that define modern rail travel and cargo shipping.

The Rise of the New York Central Railroad

Cornelius Vanderbilt's New York Central Railroad was, at its peak, the largest and most powerful transportation network in the United States. The NYC connected several major cities, including New York, Albany, Buffalo, and Chicago, enabling rapid transportation of both passengers and freight. The system grew by acquiring multiple smaller railroads, such as the Hudson River Railroad and the Lake Shore and Michigan Southern Railway, forming a massive network that became a critical link in the nation's industrial economy. The railroads Vanderbilt amassed were vital to the growth of American commerce and provided a model for corporate consolidation.

Through his aggressive tactics and brilliant management, Vanderbilt transformed the previously fragmented and competitive railroad industry into a cohesive network capable of supporting an emerging industrial economy. By the time of his death, his holdings in railroads and steamships had made him one of the wealthiest men in the world. His sons, particularly William Henry Vanderbilt, continued his work, expanding his influence and maintaining the dominance of the New York Central Railroad.

Transitioning into the 20th Century

As the 20th century dawned, the railroad industry began to face new challenges. The rise of automobiles and airplanes, combined with the increasing popularity of interstate highways, began to erode the monopoly of railroads over long-distance transportation. The New York Central, like many other railroads of the era, had to contend with declining passenger traffic, though freight remained a stronghold.

Despite significant technological innovations such as the introduction of electric locomotives, railroads struggled with rising competition and economic stagnation. By the 1960s, the New York Central merged with the Pennsylvania Railroad to form the Penn Central Transportation Company. This move, designed to consolidate resources and strengthen the company's market position, ended in failure due to financial mismanagement, culminating in the bankruptcy of Penn Central in 1970.

The Rise and Fall of Penn Central

The collapse of Penn Central in 1970 sent shockwaves through the railroad industry. It exposed vulnerabilities in the way large railroad companies were run and prompted the U.S. government to intervene. In 1976, the government established Conrail, a federally owned corporation tasked with taking over the bankrupt Northeast Corridor rail lines, including those previously owned by Vanderbilt's companies.

Conrail was successful in stabilizing and revitalizing the rail network, though it continued to face challenges in a market increasingly dominated by trucks, planes, and ships. The government's involvement in Conrail underscored the deep financial and operational issues facing America's railroads. Ultimately, in 1999, Conrail was privatized and sold to two major freight operators, CSX Transportation and Norfolk Southern Corporation, both of which continue to operate the most significant parts of Vanderbilt's former empire today.

CSX Corporation: A Modern Legacy

Today, CSX Corporation represents one of the primary successors of Vanderbilt's railroad empire. With a network stretching over 21,000 miles across 23 states, CSX plays a vital role in North American freight transportation. CSX's operations focus primarily on the transportation of goods such as coal, automotive products, chemicals, and consumer goods. While the company is rooted in the legacy of the New York Central Railroad, it has evolved to meet modern challenges, particularly with regards to efficiency, environmental concerns, and competition from other modes of transportation.

Under its current leadership, CSX has made significant strides in incorporating modern technology to improve efficiency and sustainability. The company has heavily invested in automation, data analytics, and predictive maintenance to optimize its operations. Additionally, CSX is working to reduce its carbon footprint, with plans to implement more energy-efficient locomotives and expand the use of alternative fuels.

Despite these advancements, CSX faces significant challenges. The rise of intermodal transportation and the increasing dominance of trucking for short-distance deliveries have eroded some of the market share for freight railroads. Moreover, the high costs of maintaining and upgrading rail infrastructure have posed ongoing financial pressures. Still, CSX remains a leader in the freight sector and is committed to sustaining its position in the industry.

Norfolk Southern Corporation: A Contender in the Industry

Another key player in the current state of Vanderbilt's railroad empire is Norfolk Southern Corporation, which emerged in 1982 from the merger of Norfolk and Western Railway and Southern Railway. The company's network extends over 19,000 miles, primarily serving the eastern United States. Like CSX, Norfolk Southern is a dominant player in the freight sector, handling significant volumes of coal, chemicals, automotive products, and other bulk commodities.

Norfolk Southern has also embraced technological advancements to modernize its operations. The company has invested heavily in infrastructure upgrades, digital technologies, and energy-efficient locomotives. Moreover, Norfolk Southern has been at the forefront of improving customer service, reducing delays, and offering more flexible and efficient shipping options. It has built a reputation for reliability and operational efficiency.

However, Norfolk Southern faces its own set of challenges, including competition from the growing trucking industry and the increasing pressures of environmental regulations. The railroad industry is also experiencing a consolidation trend, as companies seek to merge or form alliances in response to changing market dynamics. Despite these challenges, Norfolk Southern remains a key component of Vanderbilt's legacy in the American railroad industry.

Conrail's Role in the Modern Railroad Landscape

Though Conrail no longer exists as a standalone entity, its legacy continues through its integration into CSX and Norfolk Southern. Conrail's impact on the northeastern U.S. rail system was profound, helping to stabilize the industry in the wake of the Penn Central bankruptcy. The company played a crucial role in maintaining and revitalizing rail service across critical freight corridors, especially in the densely populated northeastern region.

Conrail's legacy is particularly evident in the management of key freight routes and its contributions to the modernization of the rail system. Its integration into CSX and Norfolk Southern has helped create a more efficient, streamlined freight network that continues to serve as the backbone of American industry. The technology and systems developed by Conrail have been absorbed by its successor companies, improving the overall quality of service and infrastructure.

The Modern Rail Industry: Challenges and Opportunities

The modern American rail industry faces a host of challenges, many of which have been exacerbated by the rise of alternative transportation options such as trucking and air freight. The deregulation of the trucking industry and the rapid expansion of the interstate highway system have made trucking a more competitive option for short-haul freight.

At the same time, railroads continue to serve as the most efficient option for long-distance shipping, particularly for bulk commodities. Freight trains can carry a far larger volume of goods than trucks, and rail transport is significantly more fuel-efficient than trucking. This makes railroads an attractive option for industries that require the movement of large quantities of goods over long distances.

As climate change and environmental sustainability continue to be critical concerns, railroads are well-positioned to play an integral role in the future of transportation. Modern railroads are increasingly focusing on reducing their carbon footprints, adopting energy-efficient technologies, and investing in renewable energy sources.

The future of Vanderbilt's railroad empire lies in its ability to adapt to these challenges. Railroads must balance the demands of sustainability, technological innovation, and the competitive pressures from other industries. The companies that trace their origins to Vanderbilt's vision must continue to evolve and modernize if they are to remain relevant in the global economy.

The Future of Vanderbilt's Legacy in Railroads

The legacy of Cornelius Vanderbilt's railroad empire is evident in the continued dominance of companies like CSX and Norfolk Southern. These companies have weathered the storm of changing transportation preferences and economic downturns, and they continue to evolve in response to modern needs. As the U.S. economy becomes increasingly globalized and environmentally conscious, railroads remain an essential part of the transportation mix.

Looking to the future, the railroad industry will likely see more innovation in terms of automation, energy efficiency, and digital transformation. New technologies such as autonomous trains, high-speed rail, and smart infrastructure may reshape the way railroads operate. The shift toward sustainable transportation will also present both challenges and opportunities for rail companies, as they work to reduce emissions and modernize their fleets.

Ultimately, while the specific companies that arose from Vanderbilt's original empire have changed and transformed, the influence of his vision remains deeply ingrained in the operations of modern railroads. As the world moves forward, the foundational principles laid by Cornelius Vanderbilt will continue to guide the development of the American railroad industry for years to come.

CHAPTER EIGHT

JOHN PIERPONT (J.P.) MORGAN – BANKING AND FINANCE

(The History of J.P. Morgan and His Banking Legacy)

Introduction: Foundations of J.P. Morgan's Banking Legacy

The story of J.P. Morgan is intricately tied to the development of American banking and finance. His family's roots in banking played a significant role in shaping his future as one of the most influential financiers in history. J.P. Morgan's ability to navigate turbulent economic times, foster economic development, and shape financial markets helped him build a legacy that would last for generations. Through his work, he not only played an instrumental role in stabilizing the U.S. economy but also helped establish institutions that would continue to evolve well into the 21st century. This extensive history of J.P. Morgan's firm, its evolution, and its involvement in global finance outlines the fundamental role it played in shaping modern banking and finance.

Early Years of J.P. Morgan (1837–1860s)

John Pierpont Morgan was born in 1837 in Hartford, Connecticut, into a family with deep roots in finance. His father, Junius Spencer Morgan, was a prominent banker who ran a successful firm in the United States. J.P. Morgan's exposure to the world of banking came early, as he learned the trade under his father's tutelage. After completing his formal education in Europe, J.P. Morgan returned to the United States to begin his career in finance.

He joined George Peabody & Co., a British-American investment bank, which was one of the most prominent firms in the United States at the time. During this period, Morgan made important contacts and began to learn the intricacies of international finance, which would play a crucial role in his future success. In the early 1860s, J.P. Morgan began working for his father's firm, J.S. Morgan & Co., which allowed him to build his own financial relationships and expand his expertise in investment banking.

J.P. Morgan's early career was marked by his focus on the emerging American railroad industry. Railroads were crucial to the economic development of the United States during the 19th century, and Morgan quickly recognized the opportunity to finance the construction and expansion of the nation's rail network.

Establishing J.P. Morgan & Co. (1870s–1890s)

In the 1870s, after spending years gaining experience in the finance sector, J.P. Morgan struck out on his own and founded J.P. Morgan & Co. in New York City. The firm quickly gained prominence in the growing American economy, particularly in the railroads and infrastructure sectors. At the time, the U.S. economy was in the midst of significant industrialization, and J.P. Morgan's firm became a central player in providing the capital needed to support this expansion. He financed major railroad companies and facilitated a number of mergers that led to the creation of powerful industrial monopolies.

Morgan's ability to engineer corporate mergers was legendary. One of his most significant achievements in this period was the creation of U.S. Steel, which became the world's first billion-dollar company in 1901. The consolidation of steel producers, including the renowned Carnegie Steel Company, under the umbrella of U.S. Steel, marked a key turning point in the history of American industry. The merger would not only change the landscape of the steel industry but also solidify Morgan's reputation as a master of financial engineering and consolidation.

Morgan's firm was also instrumental in financing other major industries, including utilities, mining, and banking. His ability to bring together companies from various sectors under a single financial umbrella became a hallmark of his career, cementing his influence over the growing American economy.

Crisis Management and Financial Stabilization (1890s–1913)

J.P. Morgan's influence in the world of finance reached new heights during the Panic of 1893, one of the most significant financial crises in American history. The depression led to the failure of several banks, railroads, and businesses across the U.S. During this turbulent period, J.P. Morgan played a central role in stabilizing the economy. He personally intervened to prevent further bank collapses and provided significant loans to the U.S. government to replenish its gold reserves. This was an important moment in Morgan's career, as it showcased his ability to act decisively and restore confidence in the financial system.

Morgan's influence in times of crisis was demonstrated again in the Panic of 1907, a banking crisis that resulted in widespread financial instability. During the panic, several major financial institutions faced insolvency, and stock prices plummeted. In response, J.P. Morgan took direct action, orchestrating a rescue effort that involved organizing a coalition of banks to provide liquidity and prevent further panic. Morgan's personal involvement in the crisis helped avert a complete financial collapse, and his actions led to the eventual establishment of the Federal Reserve System in 1913, which aimed to provide greater stability to the U.S. banking system.

The Federal Reserve Act, passed in response to the 1907 crisis, was an important milestone in the development of the U.S. financial system. It marked the beginning of a new era in banking, and Morgan's influence in the formation of the central banking system was profound. The Federal Reserve would provide a more consistent and reliable means of managing the country's monetary policy, preventing the sort of financial crises that had plagued the U.S. in the past.

Expansion and Influence in the Early 20th Century (1910s–1920s)

By the 1910s, J.P. Morgan & Co. had become a global financial powerhouse. Morgan's firm expanded its operations beyond the United States and began to play a key role in international finance. The company helped finance the reconstruction of Europe following World War I and was instrumental in managing loans to foreign governments. This period marked the beginning of Morgan's dominance in global finance, as the firm managed investments, issued bonds, and provided financial advisory services to companies and governments around the world.

In the 1920s, J.P. Morgan's firm helped finance major mergers and acquisitions, further solidifying its position at the center of American industry. As the U.S. economy roared into the Roaring Twenties, J.P. Morgan's firm continued to lead in financing new corporate ventures, including the expansion of the automobile industry, utilities, and telecommunications. The firm's expertise in large-scale corporate financing allowed it to maintain its prominent position in the U.S. and abroad.

The Great Depression and the Resilience of J.P. Morgan (1930s)

The Great Depression of the 1930s tested the resilience of the banking industry, and J.P. Morgan's firm was not immune to the turmoil. The stock market crash of 1929 and the subsequent economic downturn brought devastating consequences to many industries, including banking. The collapse of the banking system led to widespread unemployment, and many companies faced bankruptcy. However, despite the economic challenges, J.P. Morgan's firm managed to weather the storm.

During the Depression, J.P. Morgan continued to provide stability to the banking system. Although the firm suffered losses like other financial institutions, Morgan's leadership remained a stabilizing force in a time of unprecedented economic instability. By continuing to guide the firm through this challenging period, J.P. Morgan cemented his legacy as a financial leader capable of navigating the toughest of times.

Post-World War II Era and the Growth of J.P. Morgan (1940s–1960s)

Following World War II, J.P. Morgan & Co. expanded rapidly, both in the U.S. and internationally. As the global economy shifted, Morgan's firm helped finance the reconstruction of Europe and played a central role in facilitating the U.S. economic expansion. The firm became deeply involved in the growing world of multinational corporations, particularly as American companies expanded their operations globally.

During the 1950s and 1960s, J.P. Morgan continued to diversify its operations. The firm expanded into new areas of finance, including insurance, wealth management, and commercial banking. These expansions allowed Morgan's firm to diversify its services and create a more comprehensive financial portfolio. The firm also increasingly dealt with corporate advisory services, offering strategic guidance to major industrial companies on mergers, acquisitions, and capital management.

The Merger with Chase Manhattan Corporation (2000)

In 2000, J.P. Morgan merged with Chase Manhattan Corporation, one of the largest and most successful commercial banking institutions in the U.S. The merger created J.P. Morgan Chase & Co., a global financial giant that continues to be a dominant force in the banking world. The merger combined J.P. Morgan's strengths in investment banking with Chase's expertise in retail and commercial banking, creating a diversified financial institution capable of serving a wide range of clients, from individuals and small businesses to multinational corporations and governments.

The merger marked the culmination of years of consolidation and diversification in the banking sector, and J.P. Morgan Chase quickly became one of the world's largest financial institutions. Today, it is a leading player in investment banking, commercial banking, asset management, and private banking.

The Legacy of J.P. Morgan's Banking Empire

J.P. Morgan's history is intertwined with the development of the U.S. banking system and global finance. From his early days working in his father's firm to establishing his own financial empire, J.P. Morgan's vision and financial acumen transformed not only the American economy but also the global financial system. His ability to navigate crises, orchestrate corporate mergers, and provide strategic guidance to governments and corporations helped shape the modern financial landscape.

Today, J.P. Morgan Chase & Co. remains one of the world's most influential and powerful financial institutions, with a legacy that continues to impact the global economy.

(Rise of J.P. Morgan's Banking Empire)

J.P. Morgan's rise in the banking world represents one of the most impressive sagas of wealth accumulation, financial influence, and industrial consolidation in modern history. His banking empire spanned the globe, and his role as both a financier and a stabilizing force in times of economic uncertainty has left an indelible mark on the development of American capitalism. To understand the full scope of Morgan's rise, it is essential to examine not only the tactical steps he took but also the strategic decisions that allowed him to dominate the financial landscape and contribute to the modernization of the global economy. This comprehensive overview of his rise provides an in-depth exploration of the events, partnerships, and key decisions that defined his career.

Early Life and Formation of J.P. Morgan & Co.

J.P. Morgan was born in 1837 to Junius Spencer Morgan, a banker, and Sophia Walker Morgan, in Hartford, Connecticut. He was educated at the Boston Commercial School and briefly studied in Europe, including time at Goethe University in Frankfurt, where he was exposed to international banking and finance. His early exposure to the business world came through his father's work in London with the firm George Peabody & Co., one of the leading financial institutions at the time. It was through this connection that Morgan honed his skills in international finance and learned the importance of securing capital for major industrial projects, a skill that would serve him throughout his career.

Morgan returned to the United States in the 1860s and became involved in the family's banking business. However, it wasn't until 1871, when Morgan established his own banking firm, J.P.

Morgan & Co., that he began to make his presence felt in the financial world. At the time, the banking industry was highly fragmented, and a vast network of small, independent institutions operated across the U.S. Morgan, who already had experience in financing major projects, would ultimately make his mark by providing large-scale funding for railroads, utilities, and manufacturing corporations that were driving the American industrial revolution.

The Railroad Industry: Foundation of Morgan's Early Power

One of the key sectors where Morgan quickly established his dominance was the railroad industry. As the U.S. economy expanded, railroads became the backbone of the nation's infrastructure, enabling the transportation of goods and people across vast distances. During the late 1860s and 1870s, the railroad industry faced enormous capital demands as it sought to expand westward. This created an opportunity for financial institutions like Morgan's to provide the necessary funding to keep the industry growing.

Morgan's first significant railroad involvement came in 1871, when he began working with the Philadelphia and Reading Railroad. He quickly became an expert in financing, organizing, and restructuring railroads that had struggled due to poor management and inefficient operations. His firm was instrumental in refinancing the Erie Railroad and Northern Pacific Railway, two major lines that had been on the brink of bankruptcy. Morgan's restructuring of these railroads was a precursor to his larger strategy of corporate consolidation, where he could combine smaller companies into more efficient, profitable entities.

In 1885, Morgan orchestrated a deal to combine the Southern Pacific and Union Pacific railroads into one powerful entity. His success in restructuring these companies established him as a financial expert in railroad mergers and led to further investments in the industry. Morgan had a keen understanding of the financial mechanisms needed to stabilize and reorganize these complex enterprises. Over time, his firm became a dominant force in the railroad sector, controlling vast stretches of track and transportation infrastructure across the United States.

The Rise of Corporate Consolidation: The Creation of U.S. Steel

As the 19th century progressed, the United States entered the age of corporate consolidation. The railroad industry was just one example of how companies could be merged and streamlined to create more efficient, powerful entities. Morgan was at the forefront of this movement, applying the principles of consolidation to other industries, most notably steel.

In the late 1890s, the steel industry in the U.S. was fragmented, with many small steel companies struggling to compete with European giants like Bessemer Steel in Britain. American industry needed a stronger, more competitive steel manufacturer. Morgan recognized that a consolidation of U.S. steel assets could create a company powerful enough to compete on the world stage. This vision led to one of his most significant achievements: the creation of U.S. Steel in 1901.

In a deal that would ultimately reshape the steel industry, Morgan brought together the assets of Carnegie Steel, owned by steel magnate Andrew Carnegie, with those of several other major steel firms. The merger created the world's first billion-dollar corporation, U.S. Steel, which immediately became the largest steel producer in the world. The formation of U.S. Steel also marked the beginning of a new phase in the development of corporate America, where monopolies and trusts began to dominate entire industries. Morgan's ability to orchestrate such a monumental deal, bringing together rivals like Carnegie and other steel magnates, was a testament to his unparalleled negotiating skills and his understanding of the future of American industrial power.

The creation of U.S. Steel also highlighted Morgan's growing influence. Not only had he transformed an entire sector of the economy, but he had also gained control over a vast portion of the nation's steel production, which was a key component of industrial development, infrastructure, and military strength. The impact of U.S. Steel extended far beyond just the corporate world—it was a symbol of the growing concentration of economic power in the hands of a few key individuals, with Morgan at the helm.

Stabilizing the Economy: Morgan's Role in Financial Crises

While Morgan's rise to power was marked by corporate consolidation, his influence went far beyond industrial mergers. He was also called upon during moments of crisis, and his ability to stabilize the financial system was crucial to his rise as the leading financier of the Gilded Age.

The first major financial crisis that tested Morgan's influence came during the Panic of 1893, one of the worst economic downturns in U.S. history. A series of bank failures and stock market crashes had resulted in widespread economic instability, and the U.S. government found itself in a precarious position, with the gold reserves running dangerously low. The country was facing the very real threat of a collapse in its banking system, and public confidence was evaporating. Morgan was called upon to help restore financial stability.

In response, Morgan led negotiations for a $65 million gold loan to the U.S. government, which helped stabilize the national economy. This loan not only restored confidence in the financial system but also further cemented Morgan's role as one of the most powerful figures in American finance. His ability to step in and negotiate such an important deal showed that Morgan had not only accumulated wealth but also had the strategic foresight to act decisively in times of crisis.

Morgan's role as a stabilizing force was further demonstrated in 1907, during the Panic of 1907, when a series of bank failures and a run on the stock market threatened to plunge the U.S. into another economic depression. Once again, Morgan stepped in, using his vast network of financial relationships to coordinate a massive effort to stabilize the banking system. He personally negotiated a deal among a coalition of banks to provide emergency funds to struggling financial institutions. This act of leadership helped restore calm to the financial system and prevented a complete collapse of the banking sector. Morgan's efforts during the Panic of 1907 were widely praised, and the event ultimately led to the creation of the Federal Reserve System in 1913, which was designed to prevent such crises from happening in the future.

Expansion and Global Influence

By the early 20th century, J.P. Morgan's influence had expanded far beyond U.S. borders. Morgan understood that the interconnected nature of global finance meant that American banking institutions could no longer operate in isolation. He began forging relationships with European banks, and his firm became a key player in international finance.

Morgan's international dealings included financing projects in Latin America, Asia, and Europe, which allowed him to extend his influence across the globe. His ability to negotiate large international loans and form strategic alliances with European bankers gave him unprecedented access to foreign markets and capital. The firm's global reach was demonstrated by Morgan's role in financing various international ventures, including the construction of railroads in Latin America and the expansion of European trade networks. Morgan's vision for global economic integration helped solidify his legacy as one of the first truly global financiers.

Morgan's influence also extended into the formation of important business ventures abroad. His firm played a central role in financing the construction of the Panama Canal, a project that would significantly shorten shipping routes between the Pacific and Atlantic Oceans. This project, like many others, benefitted from Morgan's ability to leverage both financial capital and strategic partnerships.

The Peak of J.P. Morgan's Empire

By the time of his death in 1913, J.P. Morgan had solidified his position as the most powerful financier in the world. His rise had been marked by a combination of strategic mergers, financial acumen, and an ability to navigate the complexities of both national and international banking crises. Through his personal leadership and the operations of J.P. Morgan & Co., Morgan had helped shape the trajectory of U.S. industrialization, and his impact on global finance was profound.

His empire included not only railroads, steel, and utilities, but also an extensive network of international operations. Morgan's role in financial crises, his ability to consolidate industries, and his global outreach were defining features of his rise. His legacy continues through the global financial institution JPMorgan Chase, a modern-day testament to the lasting influence of his financial genius.

Morgan's rise was not just about wealth accumulation—it was about shaping the course of history, building a foundation for modern finance, and establishing principles that would guide the financial world for generations to come. His story is a complex and multi-faceted one, filled with bold moves, transformative deals, and a drive to create a lasting legacy. J.P. Morgan's influence in the world of banking remains unparalleled, and his contributions to modern capitalism are still felt today.

J.P. Morgans Death

J.P. Morgan, the influential financier and founder of J.P. Morgan & Co., passed away on March 31, 1913, at the age of 75. His death marked the end of an era in American banking, as he had been a central figure in shaping the financial landscape of the United States. Morgan's legacy as a titan of industry, who helped stabilize the U.S. economy during critical periods, including the 1907 financial panic, lives on through his firm, which later evolved into the global banking giant J.P. Morgan Chase & Co. His passing left a significant void in the world of finance, but his impact continues to resonate today.

"If you have to ask how much it costs, you can't afford it".- J.P. Morgan

(Current condition of J.P. Morgan's Empire)

J.P. Morgan Chase & Co. - Today's Conditions, Global Operations, and Future Outlook

Introduction J.P. Morgan Chase & Co., widely known simply as J.P. Morgan, stands as one of the foremost global financial institutions in the 21st century. With a legacy that stretches over 200 years, the firm has grown into an influential player in multiple sectors of finance, from investment banking and wealth management to retail banking and asset management. As of the latest reports, J.P. Morgan Chase remains the largest bank in the

United States by assets and is recognized globally for its market-leading positions across multiple lines of business. This detailed overview explores the current conditions of the company, including its financial health, global operations, technological advancements, sustainability efforts, and strategic future plans.

J.P. Morgan Chase Today: A Leading Global Financial Services Firm

As of the most recent financial statements, J.P. Morgan Chase holds over $3.7 trillion in assets, making it not only the largest financial institution in the United States but also one of the largest in the world. The company operates across 100+ countries, employing hundreds of thousands of individuals in diverse roles. Its market capitalization consistently ranks among the top financial institutions globally, reflecting the widespread investor confidence in its operations. In 2023, J.P. Morgan Chase reported revenues exceeding $130 billion, underscoring its substantial role in global finance. Despite facing various global challenges, such as geopolitical tensions, inflationary pressures, and technological disruptions, the company remains robust, demonstrating the resilience built on its diversified financial operations.

Core Business Segments

J.P. Morgan Chase operates through five key business segments, each contributing significantly to its revenue and global influence. These segments form the backbone of the firm's diverse portfolio, enabling it to offer a comprehensive range of financial services to individual customers, businesses, and institutions worldwide.

1. Consumer & Community Banking (CCB)

The Consumer & Community Banking division, which operates under the Chase brand, represents a major part of J.P. Morgan's retail banking business. This segment serves millions of individuals, small businesses, and communities, offering a wide array of products such as checking accounts, savings accounts, credit cards, auto loans, mortgages, and more. With a market-leading U.S. retail bank network, Chase operates over 5,000 branches and 16,000 ATMs across the United States.

Chase has embraced digital banking in recent years, expanding its mobile app capabilities and introducing features like Chase QuickPay, bill pay, and mobile check deposit, which cater to a new generation of tech-savvy customers. The division has been pivotal in increasing the firm's reach, both geographically and demographically, with a growing focus on digital solutions in an era of financial inclusion.

2. Corporate & Investment Bank (CIB)

The Corporate & Investment Bank (CIB) division is perhaps the most globally influential part of J.P. Morgan Chase, providing a vast range of services including investment banking, treasury services, capital markets, and financial advisory for large corporate clients, governments, and institutional investors. J.P. Morgan's investment banking division is a recognized leader in M&A advisory, debt and equity underwriting, and market-making in securities.

J.P. Morgan has maintained its top-tier status in global capital markets, frequently ranking as a lead underwriter in both debt and equity offerings, facilitating corporate debt issuance, and conducting equity trading and securities research. The company is also a key player in structured finance, offering investment and financing solutions to large institutions around the world.

Additionally, J.P. Morgan's treasury services and foreign exchange desks provide global liquidity and facilitate international transactions, making it a central player in the international financial markets.

3. Asset & Wealth Management (AWM)

With a comprehensive range of investment products and services, J.P. Morgan's Asset & Wealth Management division serves a broad spectrum of clients, including high-net-worth individuals, institutional investors, and pension funds. The division offers mutual funds, hedge funds, private equity, private banking, and retirement solutions, among others.

As of recent reports, the division manages $3.7 trillion in assets, making it one of the largest asset managers in the world. J.P. Morgan's wealth management services are highly regarded, with a significant portion of its clientele coming from affluent families, foundations, and endowments. Additionally, the company provides ESG (environmental, social, and governance) investment opportunities, allowing clients to align their investment portfolios with their values.

4. Commercial Banking (CB)

The Commercial Banking division focuses on delivering comprehensive financial solutions to small- and mid-market companies, as well as large corporations. This segment provides services like loans, treasury services, payment processing, capital raising, and merchant services.

J.P. Morgan's commercial banking group has grown substantially, especially in sectors such as technology, real estate, and energy, supporting businesses with specialized financing solutions. The division has extended its reach internationally, helping businesses expand globally by providing access to capital markets and cross-border payments.

5. Securities Services

J.P. Morgan's Securities Services division offers a broad range of investment services, including custody, clearing, fund administration, and prime brokerage. This division is instrumental in providing services to institutional clients like asset managers, hedge funds, and mutual funds, allowing them to manage risk, liquidity, and operations efficiently across global markets.

The firm's custody services, in particular, are among the largest in the industry, and it holds a leading position in providing foreign exchange and cash management services.

Global Presence and Strategic Operations

J.P. Morgan Chase's global operations extend across multiple continents, with the firm's headquarters located in New York City. However, the company has significant branches and offices in financial centers across the world. Notably, the firm has a strong presence in London, Hong Kong, Tokyo, Singapore, Frankfurt, and Sydney, catering to multinational corporations and institutional clients across the globe.

The company's Asia-Pacific operations have grown rapidly in recent years, with J.P. Morgan Chase becoming a prominent player in China, India, and other emerging markets in the region. The firm continues to strengthen its investment banking, asset management, and private equity businesses in these regions, capitalizing on the growing demand for financing, corporate advisory services, and wealth management solutions.

In addition to its established global markets, J.P. Morgan Chase has also expanded into Latin America and Africa, providing a range of services that support infrastructure, development, and economic growth in these emerging regions. The firm is heavily involved in trade finance, project financing, and social impact investing, demonstrating its commitment to supporting the growth of developing economies.

Technological Advancements: The Digital Transformation

One of the defining features of J.P. Morgan Chase's recent development is its heavy focus on technological innovation. The firm has made substantial investments in digital banking, artificial intelligence (AI), blockchain technology, and cloud computing, recognizing that technology will play a pivotal role in reshaping financial services for the future.

The company's Chase Mobile App and Chase Online Banking platform are integral to its consumer services, offering customers a seamless digital banking experience that includes mobile check deposits, bill payments, money transfers, and budgeting tools. The firm has also integrated its digital platforms with Zelle, a P2P payment network, to facilitate instantaneous fund transfers between accounts.

On the corporate banking front, J.P. Morgan has been at the forefront of utilizing blockchain technology to streamline and secure cross-border payments, launching JPM Coin, a digital token that enables instant transactions between institutional clients. This initiative reflects the company's commitment to adopting new technologies to enhance operational efficiency, security, and customer experience.

The firm also recognizes the transformative potential of cloud computing. In partnership with Amazon Web Services (AWS), J.P. Morgan is migrating its entire investment banking business to the cloud, a move expected to enhance operational agility and scalability while improving risk management and compliance capabilities.

Commitment to Sustainability and Corporate Responsibility

J.P. Morgan Chase has long recognized its role in addressing global challenges such as climate change, sustainability, and social inequality. As part of its broader mission to drive positive change, the company has committed to achieving net-zero carbon emissions by 2050.

The bank has allocated $2.5 trillion in sustainable financing over a 10-year period, focusing on projects that promote clean energy, energy efficiency, and sustainable agriculture. Additionally, J.P. Morgan Chase has taken strides to increase its financing of green bonds and social impact investments, providing capital for projects that advance environmental sustainability and foster positive social outcomes.

The firm's sustainability strategy also includes ensuring that its own operations, including office buildings and data centers, are carbon-neutral and powered by renewable energy. J.P. Morgan Chase has committed to financing renewable energy projects, aligning with its broader environmental goals.

In terms of social responsibility, J.P. Morgan Chase supports initiatives aimed at financial inclusion and economic empowerment, particularly for underserved communities. Through initiatives like AdvancingCities, the firm has committed billions to enhancing education, workforce development, and community revitalization, particularly in economically disadvantaged areas across the United States.

Strategic Future Plans

Looking ahead, J.P. Morgan Chase has outlined several key strategic priorities to sustain its leadership in the global financial services sector:

Digital Transformation: Continuing to innovate in fintech, blockchain, and AI, with a focus on enhancing client experience, security, and operational efficiency.

Sustainability: Meeting its net-zero emissions target by 2050 and scaling investments in sustainable projects and green technologies.

Global Expansion: Deepening its footprint in emerging markets like Asia, Latin America, and Africa, with a focus on inclusive growth and providing financial services to underserved populations.

Client-Centricity: Strengthening relationships with institutional clients, businesses, and consumers through personalized, tech-driven solutions tailored to their evolving needs.

J.P. Morgan Chase & Co. stands as an epitome of resilience, innovation, and global financial leadership. Today, the firm is navigating a rapidly evolving financial landscape, driven by technological advancements, changing client expectations, and an evolving regulatory environment. With a focus on sustainable growth, innovation, and financial inclusion, J.P. Morgan Chase is well-positioned to continue its leadership role in the global financial system, helping to shape the future of finance while addressing global challenges.

CHAPTER NINE

THOMAS EDISON – GENERAL ELECTRIC

(History of Thomas Edison and General Electric)

Introduction

Thomas Alva Edison's legacy as an inventor, entrepreneur, and industrialist is unparalleled. Edison's life and work stand as an embodiment of human ingenuity and perseverance. Throughout his lifetime, he developed over 1,000 patents, fundamentally changing the technological landscape. His key inventions—the phonograph, the incandescent light bulb, and the motion picture camera—revolutionized industries, impacted daily life, and paved the way for new fields of study. But perhaps one of his greatest achievements was the creation of General Electric (GE), a company that not only advanced electrical technology but also became a cornerstone of industrial development globally. General Electric's origins are deeply tied to Edison's relentless pursuit of innovation, and his vision still influences its operations today.

This detailed history of Edison and General Electric traces their intertwined paths from Edison's early life, the groundbreaking inventions that shaped his career, to the founding and evolution of General Electric, and the enduring legacy they both left. It explores the vast impact of Edison's work on the modern world, as well as GE's enduring influence in industries ranging from energy to aviation, healthcare, and more.

Early Life and Education

Birth and Family Background

Thomas Alva Edison was born on February 11, 1847, in Milan, Ohio, to Samuel Edison Jr. and Nancy Matthews Elliott. Edison was the youngest of seven children, born into a relatively poor family that moved frequently in search of better opportunities. His father, Samuel, was an ambitious but often unsuccessful businessman, and his mother, Nancy, was a teacher who had a profound influence on his early education. Edison's early years were marked by an unsettled lifestyle due to the family's constant relocation. They eventually settled in Port Huron, Michigan, where Edison's formal schooling began.

Struggles with Formal Education

Edison was a curious and restless child, but his early schooling experience was not a positive one. At the age of seven, he entered the local public school but struggled with traditional classroom structures. He was considered a poor student due to his inability to focus on rote learning and traditional methods of teaching. His teacher labeled him as "addled," a term for confused or mentally impaired, which led to his mother pulling him out of school. Edison's mother, a schoolteacher, recognized her son's potential and took it upon herself to educate him at home, offering him books on a wide range of subjects and encouraging his natural inquisitiveness.

Fostering a Love of Learning

Edison spent much of his childhood experimenting with various scientific concepts, reading about them in books and magazines. His family didn't have a lot of money, but his mother supported his interests by giving him access to books on science, literature, and history. Edison's insatiable curiosity was evident early on, as he would often dismantle household devices, trying to understand how they worked. Edison's first major experiment was setting up a small laboratory in the basement of his house, where he conducted rudimentary experiments in chemistry and physics.

By the time he was 12, Edison had begun working on the Grand Trunk Railroad in Michigan as a newsboy. This job allowed him time to read during his spare moments, and he became particularly interested in the latest scientific advancements. It was during this time that he purchased a book on chemistry, which led to more advanced self-study and experimentation.

Teenage Years and the Beginning of His Career

When Edison was 16, he left his job as a newsboy and found work as a telegraph operator. The telegraph industry at the time was growing rapidly, and Edison's understanding of electrical signals and his ability to work with them would soon make him a key figure in electrical engineering. This experience with telegraphy would later serve as a significant influence on many of his inventions.

In 1866, at the age of 19, Edison moved to Boston, where he continued to work as a telegraph operator. He quickly became known for his ability to repair and improve telegraph equipment, gaining a reputation for both his talent and his mechanical skills. By 1869, he was granted his first patent for an electrical vote recorder, though it did not succeed commercially. However, this early venture set him on the path to developing more useful and commercially viable inventions.

The Path to Invention and Early Innovations

First Major Inventions

Edison's first successful invention came in 1876, with the establishment of his famous Menlo Park Laboratory in New Jersey. Menlo Park became the birthplace of many of Edison's key inventions and was one of the world's first major industrial research laboratories. Here, Edison worked tirelessly to turn scientific ideas into practical products that could benefit society. Edison's approach to innovation was methodical and driven by his deep understanding of market needs and human desires.

One of Edison's early successes was the phonograph, invented in 1877. This groundbreaking invention could record and reproduce sound, marking the birth of the modern music industry. The phonograph was a revolutionary technology, making Edison famous worldwide and earning him the moniker of "The Wizard of Menlo Park." The phonograph was initially used for voice recording and entertainment, but it also had important applications in business and education, providing a model for the recording industry for generations to come.

The Incandescent Light Bulb and Electrical Power

Despite his success with the phonograph, Edison's most iconic achievement would come with the invention of the incandescent light bulb. By the late 1870s, various scientists had worked on electric light, but none had produced a viable commercial version. Edison's breakthrough came after years of experimentation with materials for filaments and improvements in electrical wiring. In 1879, he successfully demonstrated the first practical incandescent bulb that could burn for hours without burning out, using carbonized bamboo filament. This innovation, along with his creation of a complete electric power distribution system, laid the foundation for what would become the modern electrical power industry.

Edison's Pearl Street Station in New York City, which began operating in 1882, was the world's first central power station, supplying electricity to a limited area of Manhattan. The power station used direct current (DC) to distribute power, and Edison began laying the groundwork for the global electrification of industries, homes, and cities. Despite facing competition from other inventors and investors (most notably Nikola Tesla and George Westinghouse, who championed alternating current, or AC), Edison's DC systems remained influential for years.

The Founding of General Electric and Expansion

Edison Electric Light Company

In 1889, Edison founded the Edison General Electric Company, a venture designed to capitalize on his electrical innovations and spread electric lighting systems across the country. Edison's new company would be instrumental in bringing electricity into the homes and factories of millions of people, transforming the way people lived and worked.

The Edison Electric Light Company grew rapidly as the demand for electric lighting systems expanded. The company also began investing in the development of other electrical technologies, such as electric motors and transformers. Edison's forward-thinking vision of a world powered by electricity helped shape the company's expansion in both the U.S. and abroad.

The Formation of General Electric

In 1892, the Edison Electric Light Company merged with the Thomson-Houston Electric Company—a rival company that had developed an alternative electrical system—creating General Electric (GE). This merger solidified GE's position as a leader in the electrical industry and enabled the company to compete on a global scale. The newly formed GE became a major player in the development of electric power generation and distribution systems and quickly expanded into other industries, including electric railways and telecommunications.

Despite the merger, Edison remained involved in GE for several years, influencing its research and development strategies. His focus on technological innovation, customer needs, and practical applications became central to GE's corporate culture and guiding principles.

Later Years and Legacy

Retirement and Continued Innovation

By the turn of the century, Edison had become one of the wealthiest men in America. However, he never stopped inventing. In his later years, Edison focused on other projects, including the development of an alkaline storage battery, improvements to motion picture technology, and innovations in rubber production.

Despite stepping back from day-to-day operations at GE, Edison's influence on the company remained profound. GE's research laboratories continued to churn out world-changing technologies. X-ray machines, aircraft engines, nuclear power, and medical imaging would all become key innovations coming out of the company that Edison founded.

Death and the End of an Era

Edison's health began to decline in the early 1930s, and on October 18, 1931, he passed away at the age of 84 in his home in West Orange, New Jersey. Edison's death marked the end of an era in American innovation, but his legacy lived on. He left behind a profound impact on modern life, from the widespread adoption of electric lighting to the global reach of his company, General Electric.

Edison's death did not diminish the influence of his work. In fact, his death only reinforced his status as one of the most important inventors in history. Following his death, GE continued to thrive, cementing its role as one of the largest and most successful multinational conglomerates in the world.

The Legacy of Thomas Edison and General Electric

Thomas Edison's influence continues to shape the world. His company, General Electric, which he helped to establish, has grown into one of the world's most successful multinational corporations, with significant operations in energy, aviation, healthcare, renewable energy, and additive manufacturing. The company remains a symbol of innovation, constantly adapting to new technological challenges.

Edison's legacy as an inventor and businessman goes beyond his individual patents. His approach to innovation, his ability to recognize practical applications for scientific discoveries, and his understanding of the market's needs have left an indelible mark on the world. His work laid the foundation for modern electricity and electrification and fostered a culture of technological progress that persists today.

General Electric, continuing to this day, stands as a testament to Edison's pioneering spirit, and his company remains a beacon of progress, one of the cornerstones of American industrialism, and a constant reminder of the incredible power of human creativity and persistence.

"Genius is one percent inspiration; ninety-nine percent perspiration."-Thomas Edision

(Rise of Thomas Edison and General Electric)

The Rise of Edison's Business Ventures: A Detailed Account of His Entrepreneurial Success

Thomas Edison's rise to fame and fortune wasn't just a result of his prolific inventions and scientific ingenuity; it was largely driven by his exceptional business sense and his ability to turn his groundbreaking discoveries into commercial successes. Edison's journey from an ambitious inventor to the head of a global industrial empire serves as a testament to his skill in both technology and business strategy. Although his path was fraught with challenges and early failures, it was through these experiences that Edison learned to commercialize his ideas, turning them into products that revolutionized entire industries.

From Inventor to Entrepreneur: The Birth of Edison's Business Mindset

Edison's path to commercial success was not immediate. In fact, his early life as an inventor was filled with trial and error, many of which led to financial instability. Despite his early struggles, Edison had an undeniable drive to make his inventions profitable, which was evident from the 1870s onward. His transition from merely creating innovative devices to building robust businesses that could support his ventures began when he moved to New York City. There, he encountered a wealth of financial backers who were keen to invest in his inventions.

One of Edison's first commercial successes was the development of a stock ticker, which he sold to the Gold and Stock Telegraph Company for $40,000—a substantial amount in the late 19th century. This transaction provided Edison with the necessary capital to fund future inventions, including his work on electric lighting. Edison's ability to secure funding for his ventures was pivotal to his rise, as it allowed him to push his research forward without financial constraints.

Edison Electric Light Company: Revolutionizing the Electric Industry

The turning point in Edison's business career came in 1878 when he founded the Edison Electric Light Company with the goal of developing a commercially viable electric light bulb. Although many inventors were working on incandescent lighting at the time, Edison distinguished himself by focusing on the improvement of the filament's durability and the creation of a vacuum inside the bulb, which increased its longevity and efficiency. This technological leap gave Edison the edge he needed to lead the electric lighting revolution.

Edison's electric light bulb became the hallmark of his success. However, he recognized that creating a light bulb was only one part of the equation. To truly revolutionize the world, he needed to build the infrastructure that would power homes and businesses with electricity. This led to the construction of the first electrical power station on Pearl Street in New York City in 1882. This station provided electricity to a small area of Manhattan and served as a proof of concept for the large-scale use of electrical power, cementing Edison's position as a pioneer in the field of electric power generation.

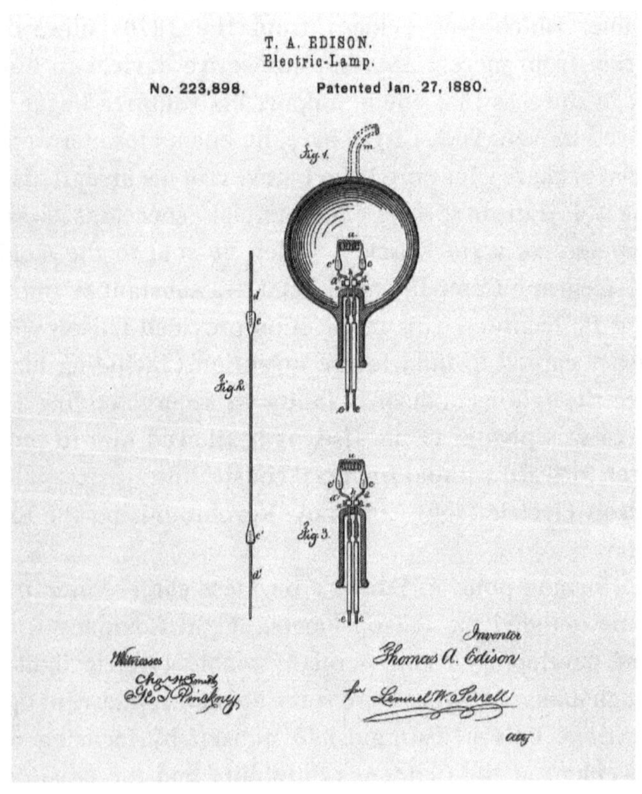

The Formation of General Electric: A Legacy Cemented

Edison's entrepreneurial spirit didn't stop at electric lighting. As his business grew, he sought to expand the scope of his company's offerings. The growth of the Edison Electric Light Company was accelerated by mergers with other companies in the electrical industry. In 1889, Edison's company merged with the Thomson-Houston Electric Company, another major player in the electrical sector, forming the General Electric Company (GE). This merger combined Edison's cutting-edge inventions with Thomson-Houston's expertise in electric motors and dynamos, enabling GE to become a diversified powerhouse in the electrical industry.

The formation of GE also helped solidify Edison's legacy, positioning the company as one of the world's first major conglomerates with a global presence. This marked the beginning of GE's transition from a company focused solely on light bulbs to a multinational corporation with a wide range of industrial products, including power generation systems, electric motors, and other electrical equipment. Edison's ability to think beyond the light bulb and focus on the broader infrastructure needed to support electricity generation laid the foundation for the company's success.

Expanding Horizons: Edison's Diverse Ventures

As GE continued to grow, Edison's role as an inventor and entrepreneur extended far beyond electric power systems. In the late 19th and early 20th centuries, Edison expanded into several groundbreaking industries, each contributing to GE's rise as a global industrial giant.

The Phonograph and Sound Recording: The Birth of the Music Industry

Edison's invention of the phonograph in 1877 was one of his most notable achievements. Although the phonograph was initially a commercial failure, it eventually revolutionized the music and entertainment industries. Edison's ability to see potential in his inventions even after initial setbacks was one of his key strengths. He formed the Edison Speaking Phonograph Company, which was later absorbed into General Electric, and the phonograph became an integral part of GE's portfolio.

Edison's development of the phonograph also laid the groundwork for future technological innovations in sound recording. The phonograph eventually found applications far beyond music, becoming a valuable tool in industries like record-keeping and dictation, further expanding GE's reach.

Motion Pictures: Edison's Influence on the Film Industry

Another key area in which Edison made significant contributions was the motion picture industry. Edison developed the Kinetoscope, a device for viewing moving pictures, and went on to create the world's first motion picture studio in West Orange, New Jersey. While Edison's direct involvement in filmmaking dwindled over time, his patents and innovations in film technology played a pivotal role in the development of the modern film industry.

Edison's contributions to the motion picture industry also aligned with his broader strategy of diversification. By tapping into the rapidly growing film industry, GE was able to capitalize on new technologies and expand into the burgeoning field of entertainment. Edison's role in shaping the motion picture industry not only demonstrated his visionary business acumen but also highlighted his ability to identify emerging industries that would have lasting global impact.

Expanding the Industrial Landscape: GE's Technological and Global Growth

By the early 20th century, General Electric had grown into a diversified industrial conglomerate, and Edison's innovations continued to drive the company's success. One of the most significant ways GE contributed to industrial growth was through the application of electrical power to manufacturing processes. The development of electric motors allowed factories to increase productivity and reduce reliance on traditional mechanical power sources, ushering in a new era of industrial automation.

Edison's influence on GE extended beyond the U.S. as the company began to expand internationally. GE built factories and formed partnerships in Europe, South America, and Asia, cementing its status as a global leader in electrical and industrial technologies. The company's expansion into international markets helped GE tap into new sources of growth, particularly as demand for electricity and industrial products surged worldwide.

The Battle of Currents: A Turning Point in GE's History

One of the most dramatic moments in Edison's business journey occurred during the "Battle of the Currents" in the late 1880s and early 1890s. Edison's preference for direct current (DC) electricity was pitted against the alternating current (AC) systems championed by his rival, George Westinghouse. While Edison's DC system was initially more widely used, AC proved to be more efficient for long-distance electricity transmission and ultimately became the global standard. Despite the loss of this battle, Edison's involvement in the debate had far-reaching consequences. It led GE to adopt both AC and DC technologies, positioning the company to meet diverse energy needs and further solidifying its market leadership.

The Evolution of General Electric: Beyond Edison's Era

As Edison's health declined, he gradually withdrew from the day-to-day operations of General Electric, but by then, his vision for the company had already been realized. Under the leadership of his successors, GE expanded further, entering new industries such as aviation, military technologies, and medical devices. Edison's influence remained evident in the company's culture of innovation and entrepreneurship, and GE continued to grow into one of the most influential industrial conglomerates in the world.

General Electric's diversification strategy, initiated by Edison, allowed the company to weather economic downturns and adapt to changing technological landscapes. As a result, GE remains a global leader in energy, aviation, healthcare, and other industries, and Edison's legacy continues to live on in the company's innovative approach to business.

The Long-Term Impact of Edison's Business Acumen

Thomas Edison's entrepreneurial vision and his ability to commercialize cutting-edge technologies not only shaped the development of General Electric but also transformed entire industries worldwide. Through his inventions, Edison's influence extended from the electric power sector to entertainment, manufacturing, and beyond. His strategic focus on building infrastructures, creating industrial applications for electricity, and diversifying into new industries laid the foundation for GE's enduring global success.

Today, General Electric stands as a testament to Edison's lasting impact, continuing to drive innovation across various sectors. While Edison's direct involvement with the company ended with his death in 1931, his business acumen and entrepreneurial legacy continue to influence GE's operations and shape the world we live in. Edison once remarked, "Genius is one percent inspiration and ninety-nine percent perspiration," and his journey from inventor to business magnate exemplifies this philosophy. His ability to merge invention with entrepreneurship created a company that not only changed the way we use electricity but also reshaped industries worldwide.

(The Present Status of General Electric (GE)

Company Overview and Current Structure

General Electric (GE), founded by Thomas Edison and officially incorporated in 1892, has developed into a major multinational conglomerate with significant operations in diverse industries. Over recent decades, GE has shifted its strategy to focus on its core strengths in aviation, energy (including renewable energy), and healthcare. This strategic realignment has allowed GE to remain competitive in an ever-evolving global marketplace while adapting to current industry trends and customer demands.

GE's modern transformation has involved difficult but necessary decisions, including divesting from non-core operations, restructuring business units, and investing heavily in cutting-edge technology and sustainability initiatives. The company has streamlined its operations to concentrate on high-growth sectors and improve overall efficiency, ensuring that GE is positioned to be a leader in the industries it prioritizes.

Leadership and Management

As of 2024, H. Lawrence Culp Jr. serves as the Chairman and CEO of General Electric. Culp's appointment in 2018 marked a pivotal moment in GE's history. He was the first outsider to take the reins at GE and brought with him a reputation for transformative leadership, honed during his tenure as CEO at Danaher Corporation. Culp's management style focuses on operational rigor, lean management practices, and a strong emphasis on financial discipline.

Under Culp's leadership, GE has taken significant steps to regain its financial footing and enhance productivity. One of the most impactful moves during his tenure was the spin-off of GE HealthCare in early 2023, which allowed the healthcare division to operate as an independent, publicly traded company. This strategic decision not only strengthened GE's focus on industrial manufacturing but also allowed GE HealthCare to pursue its path in medical imaging, diagnostics, and digital health technology. Both GE and GE HealthCare have thrived as a result, each focusing on specialized markets with greater agility.

Culp has also been a champion of partnerships and technological integration. Under his direction, GE has expanded its use of digital twin technology, advanced analytics, and IoT platforms to optimize operations and enhance productivity across all divisions.

Current Divisions and Major Operations

GE Aerospace (formerly GE Aviation): GE Aerospace is a cornerstone of the company, recognized for its global leadership in aircraft engine design and manufacturing. This division provides engines and systems for commercial, military, and business aircraft, with notable clients including Boeing and Airbus. In recent years, GE Aerospace has continued to innovate with the development of fuel-efficient turbine engines that reduce emissions. Significant R&D investments have gone into exploring sustainable aviation fuel (SAF) and next-generation propulsion systems, showcasing GE's commitment to advancing environmentally friendly solutions in aviation.

GE Vernova (Energy and Renewable Energy): GE Vernova is GE's energy division, encompassing GE Gas Power, GE Steam Power, GE Renewable Energy, and GE Grid Solutions. This segment is crucial for the global power infrastructure, contributing to both traditional and renewable energy sources. GE Renewable Energy is a leader in wind energy, with flagship projects such as the Haliade-X offshore wind turbine, one of the most powerful and efficient wind turbines in the world. GE Vernova also invests in grid modernization, ensuring that electrical distribution systems are capable of supporting renewable energy and increasing overall energy reliability.

Digital Solutions and Additive Manufacturing: Beyond its primary divisions, GE has leveraged digital solutions to enhance its competitive advantage. The integration of digital twin technology allows GE to simulate and predict the performance of products throughout their life cycle, leading to improved efficiency and reduced downtime for clients. GE Additive, a separate unit, focuses on 3D printing technology to create complex parts more efficiently and cost-effectively than traditional manufacturing methods. This technology is applied across various industries, including aerospace and healthcare, reinforcing GE's status as a technological leader.

Recent Achievements and Milestones

Sustainability Commitments: GE has taken significant strides in its environmental initiatives, setting ambitious targets such as achieving carbon neutrality by 2030 across its operations and aiming for net-zero emissions by 2050. These commitments are supported by advancements in renewable energy solutions, such as offshore wind power and sustainable aviation technologies.

Technological Advancements in Aerospace: GE Aerospace has maintained its leadership by rolling out innovative products like the GE9X engine, which powers Boeing's 777X aircraft and is recognized as one of the most fuel-efficient jet engines available. Ongoing research into hybrid-electric propulsion and hydrogen-powered engines is setting the stage for the future of aviation.

Healthcare Innovations: Even after the spin-off, GE HealthCare has been a leader in advancing medical technology, focusing on AI-driven diagnostics, advanced imaging equipment, and personalized medicine. These innovations continue to position GE HealthCare as a global leader in the healthcare industry.

Properties and Global Expansion

GE's global presence extends to operations in more than 170 countries, with significant manufacturing plants, research centers, and service facilities. One of its notable research hubs, the GE Research Center in Niskayuna, New York, serves as the heart of innovation for the company, where new technologies in power generation, aviation, and healthcare are developed.

In recent years, GE has increased its investments in high-growth markets, particularly in Asia and Africa, to support renewable energy projects and expand its industrial reach. These efforts have diversified GE's revenue streams and aligned the company with the growing demand for sustainable energy solutions in emerging markets.

Financial Performance and Market Position

Following a challenging period in the late 2010s marked by financial losses and high debt, GE has shown signs of recovery. The spin-offs and strategic focus on core areas have contributed to improved profitability and reduced debt levels. GE Vernova and GE Aerospace have emerged as key revenue drivers, supported by strong demand for sustainable energy solutions and advanced aviation technologies.

GE's stock performance has seen fluctuations, but investor confidence has been bolstered by Culp's successful execution of restructuring plans. The company has regained its reputation for engineering excellence and operational capability, positioning itself as a leader in industrial technology.

Future Outlook

Looking ahead, GE's focus remains on continued innovation, sustainability, and global growth. Strategic partnerships with leading tech companies and research institutions will support its development in AI, machine learning, and sustainable technologies. GE's long-term goals include expanding its portfolio of environmentally friendly products, enhancing its digital service offerings, and maintaining its leadership in aerospace technology.

Part 3: Industry Visionaries

In this section, we explore the stories of business magnates whose enterprises have left an indelible mark on their respective industries. These individuals, coming from a variety of backgrounds and industries, share a common thread: their unyielding determination to create businesses that not only transformed their sectors but also reshaped global commerce. Each of these leaders navigated the challenges of their time, leveraging innovation, resilience, and bold decisions to build legacies that continue to thrive today.

CHAPTER TEN

GEORGE EASTMAN – EASTMAN KODAK COMPANY

(History of George Eastman and Eastman Kodak Company)

Introduction: The Origins of George Eastman and Eastman Kodak

George Eastman, the founder of Eastman Kodak Company, was one of the most pivotal figures in the history of photography and the broader world of technology. His innovations reshaped the way we capture moments and gave rise to a company that would dominate the photography industry for over a century. This history of George Eastman and the Eastman Kodak Company is a fascinating journey of invention, entrepreneurship, and foresight.

Early Life of George Eastman

George Eastman was born on July 12, 1854, in Waterville, New York, to George Washington Eastman and Maria Kilbourn Eastman. His father, a successful entrepreneur, passed away when George was just 8 years old, leaving his mother to raise him and his siblings. The family faced financial difficulties, and Eastman's early life was marked by a strong sense of responsibility and a deep desire to improve his circumstances. Despite the challenges of his youth, Eastman's education was crucial to his intellectual development. He attended local schools, showing a keen interest in mechanics and business from a young age.

After the death of his father, Eastman began working at a variety of jobs to support his family. He worked as a bank clerk, which provided him with some exposure to the business world. However, it was his exposure to photography that would ultimately lead him to pursue his true passion. In the mid-1870s, Eastman became interested in photography, a burgeoning field that at the time was both complicated and costly. Photography in the 19th century was an art reserved for the elite—an expensive process that required bulky equipment, glass plates, and extensive knowledge of chemicals and development techniques.

The Invention of Dry Plates and the Birth of Eastman Kodak

In 1877, after a few years of experimenting with various photographic methods, George Eastman made a significant breakthrough. He developed a dry plate process that replaced the earlier wet plate process, which required photographers to prepare and use glass plates while still wet. This was a cumbersome and time-consuming task that made photography impractical for most people. The dry plate process allowed photographs to be developed at a later time, making the practice more convenient.

Eastman's innovation in photography was not merely about the technical process; it also involved his vision for democratizing the art of capturing moments. Photography at the time was seen as a complex, inaccessible process reserved for professionals, with equipment and materials that were expensive and difficult to handle. Eastman believed that photography could be made accessible to everyone, not just those with professional training or considerable financial resources.

To achieve this, Eastman embarked on an ambitious mission to simplify the process of taking pictures and make photography as easy as using a consumer product. In 1880, he founded the Eastman Dry Plate Company, which would later become the Eastman Kodak Company. One of his earliest key inventions was the flexible roll film—a significant innovation in the photography industry. This film was far easier to use than glass plates, and it became the foundation for Kodak's future success. This was the starting point for Eastman Kodak's journey toward becoming a global leader in the photography industry.

The Formation of Eastman Kodak Company

In 1888, George Eastman introduced the first Kodak camera to the public. It was a groundbreaking product, designed to be easy to use for people who had no previous knowledge of photography. The camera was preloaded with film that could take up to 100 photographs before it needed to be sent to Kodak for developing and reloading. The slogan "You press the button, we do the rest" became iconic, as it highlighted the simplicity and ease of use that Kodak cameras provided. The idea was simple yet revolutionary: the consumer could take photographs without the burden of knowing how to develop the film or operate complicated equipment. Kodak handled the difficult part of the process, which opened up the world of photography to the masses.

The introduction of the Kodak camera made a significant impact. It was a small, portable device, far more convenient than the large, cumbersome cameras and glass plates that had been used previously. With this product, Eastman Kodak quickly became synonymous with photography. The company not only made cameras but also made the film itself, which could be used by consumers and professionals alike. The Kodak camera's success was fueled by Eastman's keen sense of marketing, and the company saw rapid growth in the early years.

In 1889, Eastman officially changed the company's name to Eastman Kodak Company. This name reflected the focus on simplicity, as "Kodak" was a completely made-up word that Eastman felt had a catchy, memorable sound. The brand name Kodak would go on to become one of the most recognizable in the world, synonymous with photography itself.

Early Challenges and Innovations

Despite the early success of the Kodak camera, Eastman and his company faced a number of challenges. Photography was still in its infancy, and many people were skeptical about the practicality of photography as a consumer product. The equipment, film, and developing processes were still evolving, and Eastman had to constantly innovate to stay ahead of the competition.

One of the most significant early challenges was the need for a mass production facility that could meet the increasing demand for Kodak cameras and film. Eastman understood that scaling production was essential for success, and he invested heavily in factory infrastructure. In 1892, he built a new factory in Rochester, New York, which became the heart of Kodak's operations. This factory helped Kodak meet the growing demand for photographic products and ensured that the company could continue to innovate and develop new products at a rapid pace.

Another important early innovation was Eastman's decision to create a vertically integrated supply chain. Kodak not only produced cameras and film but also controlled the entire process from manufacturing the raw materials to developing the film. This gave the company complete control over quality and cost, which helped Kodak maintain its competitive advantage.

Kodak's success was also bolstered by Eastman's commitment to research and development. He established an extensive research department, which worked on improving film quality, camera design, and the overall photographic process. In the early 1900s, Kodak introduced a series of new products that enhanced the quality of photography and made the process even more accessible. The company's cameras became smaller, lighter, and more efficient, while the film produced by Kodak became more durable and offered better resolution.

George Eastman's Vision for the Future

George Eastman's vision for Kodak was not limited to the success of his company in the photographic industry. He saw the potential for Kodak to become a dominant force in the global market, and he made strategic decisions that would lay the foundation for long-term success. Eastman understood that the photography industry was not just about selling cameras—it was about creating an entire ecosystem that included cameras, film, paper, and development services. Kodak's business model was not just to create a great product but to create a complete photographic experience for consumers.

Eastman's vision was also global. Kodak's success was not confined to the United States, and the company quickly expanded its operations worldwide. By the early 1900s, Kodak had established offices and factories in Europe, Asia, and other parts of the world. This global expansion allowed Kodak to take advantage of new markets and increase its customer base.

Eastman's ability to see the bigger picture was a key factor in Kodak's long-term success. He was constantly looking for ways to expand Kodak's product line and explore new markets. In the early 1900s, Kodak introduced new products like motion picture film and color film, which would go on to revolutionize the film and entertainment industries.

Philanthropy and Legacy

Throughout his life, George Eastman was known for his philanthropy. He believed that business success carried a responsibility to give back to society. Eastman's charitable endeavors focused on education, public health, and the arts. He made significant contributions to the University of Rochester, where the Eastman School of Music was established in his honor, and he also donated large sums to hospitals and other institutions.

Eastman's philanthropic work is a testament to his belief in the power of business to improve society. His generosity helped shape the cultural and educational landscape of the United States, and his legacy continues to impact the world today.

George Eastman's life and the history of the Eastman Kodak Company are a story of innovation, perseverance, and vision. From humble beginnings, Eastman built a company that transformed the photography industry and changed the way people interacted with images. Kodak's success was not just about creating better cameras or better film—it was about making photography accessible to the masses and creating a global brand that would stand the test of time. Eastman's innovations continue to influence the world of photography, film, and technology, and his legacy remains an integral part of the modern world.

George Eastman's Death and Legacy

George Eastman passed away on March 14, 1932, at the age of 77, at his home in Rochester, New York. His death was the result of a self-inflicted gunshot wound, and it is believed to have been driven by his struggle with chronic pain from a spinal condition, along with a deep sense of personal sadness following the loss of his mother and other life challenges. His passing marked the end of an era for Kodak and for the broader photography industry. Despite his death, George Eastman's legacy lived on through his groundbreaking contributions to the photographic world, his transformative vision for mass-market cameras, and his lasting impact on technology and philanthropy. The Eastman Kodak Company continued to thrive for decades, and Eastman's philanthropic endeavors left an indelible mark on education and healthcare. His name remains synonymous with innovation in photography, and his work laid the foundation for much of the visual culture we experience today.

"The progress of the world depends almost entirely upon education."-George Eastman

(Rise of George Eastman and Eastman Kodak Company)

The story of the rise of George Eastman and his company, Eastman Kodak, is a monumental narrative of how a small idea, through innovation, vision, and perseverance, transformed an entire industry and, ultimately, the way people lived their lives. George Eastman's journey from a young boy with modest beginnings to one of the world's most influential entrepreneurs has made Kodak synonymous with photography. The company's rise is not just a business success story, but a reflection of how Eastman revolutionized photography, democratized the process of capturing memories, and ultimately shaped the course of visual culture and personal documentation.

Early Obstacles and the First Breakthrough

As an aspiring young man in the late 19th century, Eastman was keenly aware that the art of photography was complex, expensive, and out of reach for most people. Cameras were large, cumbersome, and difficult to operate, requiring professional skills and specialized equipment. In fact, photography at that time was something only a small, affluent demographic could afford. Eastman, ever the visionary, believed that there was an untapped market for a more accessible form of photography.

Initially, Eastman's business efforts were slow to take off. The early years of Eastman Kodak were marked by substantial trial and error. Kodak's founder had a strong sense of business acumen, but he had to navigate a highly competitive and highly technical industry that was still in its infancy. He made a series of investments into research and development that were critical in the company's eventual breakthrough. One of the most important steps was Eastman's decision to shift away from glass plates to flexible roll film, which proved to be a game-changer.

The invention of roll film in 1884 was a crucial development. For decades, photographers had been using heavy glass plates, which were unwieldy and prone to breakage. Eastman's flexible film offered several advantages: it was much lighter, easier to handle, and most importantly, it allowed photographers to take multiple images on the same roll of film. With this invention, Eastman created the foundation for his vision of simplifying photography for the masses.

The Kodak Camera: A Revolutionary Product

In 1888, Eastman launched the Kodak camera — the first camera that was designed to be simple, portable, and easy to use. The camera came pre-loaded with a roll of film capable of taking 100 photographs. The groundbreaking feature was the simplicity of the camera itself: you just had to press a button, and Kodak would develop the film for you. This innovation eliminated the need for a darkroom and complex chemical knowledge, essentially making photography as easy as taking a snapshot.

The slogan, "You press the button, we do the rest," resonated with the public and was one of the most successful marketing campaigns in the history of consumer products. Kodak's camera, priced at $25, was affordable for many middle-class families and even children, which helped Kodak's products find their way into nearly every American home. The accessibility of the camera and the ease of the process turned photography from a professional pursuit into a popular, everyday hobby.

The launch of the Kodak camera marked the beginning of a new era for photography. It was an instant success, not only because of the product's simplicity but because Eastman had effectively created a consumer market for photography — something that had never existed before. Kodak's products were marketed to amateur photographers, and it quickly became clear that Eastman's vision of empowering ordinary people to capture their lives in pictures had struck a chord.

George Eastman

Expansion and Growth: Creating a Brand

The success of the Kodak camera quickly expanded beyond the borders of the United States. Eastman, ever the strategist, recognized the potential of a global market for his products. By the 1890s, Kodak had expanded its reach to Europe, Asia, and Latin America. Kodak's cameras were soon found in the hands of people all over the world, with the company's growing presence establishing Kodak as the undisputed leader in photography.

Eastman's understanding of consumer psychology and marketing techniques helped propel Kodak into the international spotlight. Kodak wasn't just a product — it was a lifestyle. Eastman envisioned Kodak as a part of the family experience, a way for people to capture their precious memories. This emotional appeal, combined with the functionality of the camera, made Kodak synonymous with photography itself.

Another key element of Kodak's rise was Eastman's approach to vertical integration. Eastman didn't just build cameras; he controlled every aspect of the photographic process. From film production to the development of pictures, Kodak had complete control over the entire process. This vertical integration allowed Kodak to maintain high-quality standards and keep costs down, giving the company a competitive edge.

The Brownie Camera: Making Photography Even More Accessible

In 1900, Kodak introduced the Brownie camera — a small, affordable, and easy-to-use camera aimed at children and amateur photographers. The Brownie was priced at just $1, making it an accessible product for even the most modest of families. This product was pivotal in Kodak's continued expansion and is considered one of the most important innovations in the history of consumer electronics.

The Brownie camera not only solidified Kodak's place in the world of personal photography, but it also created an entirely new market segment — the mass-market consumer camera. The camera was marketed with the idea that anyone could be a photographer, regardless of their social class, and it was designed to appeal to the youngest audiences. By introducing the Brownie, Eastman made photography even more democratic and helped make Kodak a household name across the globe.

Kodak's rise was not just the result of product innovation but also a result of its pioneering marketing campaigns. Eastman's keen understanding of branding allowed Kodak to appeal to both amateur and professional photographers, creating a loyal customer base that spanned generations. Kodak's use of print advertising, billboards, and innovative in-store displays helped cement its place as a dominant force in the photographic industry.

The Global Expansion and Dominance of Kodak

By the early 20th century, Eastman Kodak had grown into a global powerhouse. Kodak was operating in countries across the globe, and its products were considered the gold standard in photography. Eastman's investment in research and development continued to pay dividends, with Kodak regularly introducing new products and technologies, including color film and innovations in motion picture technology.

Throughout the 1920s and 1930s, Kodak maintained its market dominance through its commitment to innovation. Kodak expanded its product line to include films, printing papers, and other accessories that made it easier for people to engage with photography. As a result, Kodak was able to control the entire photographic ecosystem, from taking the picture to developing and printing it.

Eastman's ability to create such an extensive ecosystem around photography made Kodak an indispensable part of everyday life for millions of people. Kodak cameras and films were used by both amateur photographers and professionals, with the company also becoming an essential player in the world of professional photography and cinema. The company even expanded into the movie industry, providing film stock for Hollywood's burgeoning film studios.

The Legacy of George Eastman and Kodak's Dominance

By the 1920s and 1930s, Kodak had firmly entrenched itself as the undisputed leader in the photography industry. The company was virtually synonymous with photography, and Eastman had become one of the wealthiest and most influential men in the world. Through his philanthropy, Eastman supported a variety of causes, including the establishment of educational institutions, hospitals, and medical research foundations.

Eastman's influence extended far beyond the business world. His contributions to science and technology, his advocacy for the arts, and his philanthropic efforts set a standard for corporate responsibility and social engagement. At the time of his death in 1932, George Eastman's legacy was secure, and Kodak remained one of the most important companies in the world.

Kodak's legacy was built on Eastman's groundbreaking vision of making photography accessible to everyone. By transforming photography from a complex, expensive, and niche pursuit into a universal activity, Eastman and Kodak changed the way people interacted with the world around them. Kodak's rise was an incredible journey of innovation, branding, and corporate strategy, and it left an indelible mark on the history of technology and culture.

Through its success, Kodak made photography a part of everyday life, shaping the visual documentation of history for generations to come. Eastman's work laid the foundation for the visual culture that defines the modern world, making Kodak a symbol of memory, personal experience, and, above all, the power of visual storytelling. Kodak was not merely a company but a revolution that forever altered the way people captured, remembered, and shared their most cherished moments.

(Kodak's Current Status)

A Deeper Dive into its Present-Day Operations, Challenges, and Future Trajectory

Eastman Kodak's current position in the business world is a far cry from the industry-shaping giant it once was in the film and photography sector. However, the company has managed to survive decades of technological upheaval and dramatic shifts in consumer behavior by adapting to the ever-evolving landscape of industry and innovation. Despite these challenges, Kodak has steadily transformed itself into a diversified technology company, focusing on key sectors like digital printing, materials, chemical technology, intellectual property licensing, and more recently, pharmaceuticals and blockchain technology.

Kodak's Business Operations Today

As of the latest updates, Kodak is a publicly traded company with its headquarters still located in Rochester, New York. The company's operations today are organized into several core segments, each of which contributes to its overall financial health and strategic goals. Here's a closer look at the most important divisions within Kodak's structure:

Digital Printing and Industrial Solutions: Kodak has shifted its focus from traditional photography to digital printing, leveraging its heritage in imaging technology. The company is a key player in the commercial and industrial printing sector, where it supplies high-quality digital printing presses, imaging solutions, and prepress technology. Kodak's product portfolio includes systems like the Kodak Prosper inkjet press, which is widely used for high-volume, commercial printing, including direct mail, packaging, and publishing applications. Kodak's Kodak Nexpress digital color presses are also widely used for short-run, high-quality commercial printing.

Kodak's printing solutions have continued to find success, especially in the rapidly growing packaging industry, where demand for customized, digital packaging solutions is on the rise.

Kodak's printing innovations cater to a wide variety of sectors, from consumer goods and electronics packaging to high-end graphics and labels.

Advanced Materials and Chemicals: Kodak's early focus on chemicals and imaging materials continues to play a pivotal role in its current operations. The company produces a range of advanced chemicals used in industries beyond imaging, such as electronics, semiconductors, and batteries. Kodak's materials are also used in the manufacture of high-tech displays, where it supplies organic light-emitting diode (OLED) materials and other critical components. The company has a rich portfolio of proprietary materials used for imaging, film, and display technologies, allowing it to maintain a presence in highly specialized and growing markets.

One example of Kodak's chemical work is the development of Kodak's Digital Print technology, which is used to produce quality printed materials at a reduced cost, compared to traditional methods. Furthermore, Kodak's ongoing development of nanomaterials and materials for advanced displays signals the company's commitment to providing innovative solutions in high-demand industries.

Intellectual Property & Licensing: A major strength of Kodak today is its extensive intellectual property portfolio. The company owns thousands of patents related to imaging technologies, digital photography, and other cutting-edge innovations, including technologies for 3D printing and blockchain. Kodak has continued to generate significant revenue from licensing its patents, often entering into lucrative agreements with major tech companies, including Apple, Samsung, and Google.

Kodak's IP licensing model has become one of the company's most important business pillars. The company has capitalized on its patents, licensing them for a variety of industries beyond photography. Kodak's innovations in imaging, image processing, and digital technology remain highly valuable, and the company is actively seeking new opportunities to monetize its patent portfolio, especially in sectors where it has historically held expertise.

Pharmaceuticals and Blockchain: In a surprising strategic move, Kodak expanded into the pharmaceutical industry in 2020, when it was awarded a $765 million loan by the U.S. government as part of an effort to reshore pharmaceutical manufacturing in the United States. This loan was part of Kodak's attempt to build a facility capable of producing active pharmaceutical ingredients (APIs), including ingredients necessary for drug production. This new direction aimed to leverage Kodak's extensive manufacturing capabilities and its expertise in materials science.

Additionally, Kodak has ventured into blockchain technology through its KodakOne platform, which uses blockchain to manage digital image rights and licensing. The KodakOne platform was designed to help photographers and creatives manage their images by protecting their copyrights through blockchain-based solutions. The company's focus on blockchain reflects its efforts to adapt to new digital business models and find ways to capitalize on the growing digital asset management market.

Financial Challenges and Resilience

Kodak's financial performance in recent years has been marked by volatility, with fluctuations in its stock price and revenue generation. After emerging from bankruptcy in 2013, Kodak had to reorient its financial structure and operations toward new business opportunities. However, Kodak's position as a global innovator is still under pressure as it competes against newer, more agile technology firms in various sectors.

Revenue & Profitability: Kodak's most recent reported annual revenue is in the range of $1.5 to $2 billion, a far cry from its historical highs. While this figure is relatively stable, it highlights the company's struggle to return to the market dominance it once enjoyed. The primary revenue streams for Kodak today come from its printing solutions, advanced materials, and intellectual property licensing. These segments provide the company with a degree of financial stability, even as its traditional consumer-focused business continues to fade.

Stock Price & Market Performance: Kodak's stock has experienced significant volatility over the years. After filing for bankruptcy, the company restructured and began trading publicly once again. In recent years, Kodak's stock price has seen a resurgence due to its involvement in pharmaceutical production and blockchain technologies, but it has also faced declines due to continued market competition and an inability to regain its former position in consumer imaging. As of now, Kodak's stock remains relatively low compared to its peak value, and the company remains in the midst of its pivot toward becoming a diversified technology enterprise.

Leadership and Organizational Structure Today

Kodak's leadership today is focused on driving the company forward through its digital transformation strategy. The company is led by Jim Continenza, who serves as Chairman and CEO. Continenza's leadership has been crucial in steering Kodak through its restructuring efforts and into new industries such as digital printing, blockchain, and pharmaceuticals. Under his guidance, Kodak has diversified beyond its photographic legacy and has embraced new technologies, aiming to create a more sustainable and profitable future.

Kodak operates globally with manufacturing plants, research and development facilities, and sales offices spread across North America, Europe, and Asia. The company's structure is designed to support its diversified business portfolio, with specialized teams for each of its core segments. Kodak's team of engineers, scientists, and technicians continues to drive innovation in fields such as printing technology, materials science, and chemical development.

Current Challenges and Future Plans

Despite its ongoing efforts to reinvent itself, Kodak faces a number of ongoing challenges:

Market Competition: Kodak's competition has expanded beyond traditional rivals in the photography and printing industries to include modern digital technology giants and newer, nimble players in the printing and imaging industries. Companies like Canon, HP, and Xerox remain major competitors in the commercial printing space, while digital-first tech companies have overtaken Kodak in digital imaging solutions.

Changing Consumer Demands: The decline in traditional photography and the dominance of smartphones and social media as the primary mediums for personal photography have significantly impacted Kodak's consumer business. While Kodak has successfully revived its film products to cater to the growing nostalgia for analog photography, this is a niche market and cannot be relied upon to sustain its long-term growth.

Innovation & Technological Shifts: Kodak's ongoing push into emerging technologies such as blockchain, digital printing, and pharmaceutical manufacturing is promising but not without risks. The company must continue to invest heavily in R&D to maintain its competitive edge in these new markets, particularly in pharmaceuticals and blockchain, where competition is fierce.

Financial Stability: Kodak must continue to balance its financial operations to ensure its ongoing stability. Given its past financial troubles, maintaining a sound balance sheet and managing costs will be critical in maintaining the company's position in global markets.

Looking Ahead: Kodak's Future Prospects

Kodak's strategy moving forward appears to be focused on technological diversification and digitalization. The company will continue to rely heavily on its patent portfolio, investing in new technologies like blockchain, 3D printing, and pharmaceutical manufacturing to generate future revenue streams. Kodak is committed to positioning itself as a major player in industrial printing and materials science, sectors that are expected to grow rapidly in the coming years.

In addition, Kodak is exploring new avenues to increase its relevance, such as sustainability initiatives, digital asset management, and artificial intelligence, all while continuing to serve niche markets in photography and film. Its KodakOne platform is an example of its continued investment in blockchain and digital rights management, which could play a critical role in managing intellectual property in the increasingly digital world.

Kodak's current status reflects a company that is rebuilding itself after decades of market dominance and subsequent decline. Although it no longer holds its former position as a photography giant, Kodak has adapted to changing industry trends by focusing on high-growth sectors such as digital printing, materials science, and pharmaceuticals. The company's future will depend on its ability to stay competitive in an era of rapid technological change, and its focus on leveraging intellectual property, innovation, and strategic diversification is key to its survival and potential future growth. As it moves forward, Kodak's legacy as an imaging and technology innovator may still hold relevance in the evolving digital economy.

Famous Incidents Page

(Jamsetji Nusserwanji Tata)

One of the most defining moments in the early life of Jamsetji Tata, the founder of the Tata Group, occurred during a momentous trip to the United States in 1893. This trip, while officially aimed at exploring new business ideas, turned out to be the catalyst for some of the most transformative industrial innovations in Indian history. It all began when Jamsetji attended the World's Columbian Exposition in Chicago, a grand world's fair celebrating the centennial of the United States, where he encountered the cutting-edge developments in industrial technology and business.

Encounter with the Steel Industry

During his visit to the U.S., Jamsetji had the opportunity to observe the rapid growth of the steel industry in the country, particularly in Pittsburgh, which was at the time the heart of steel manufacturing. He was introduced to the American steel magnates and taken on a tour of steel plants that were employing advanced technologies to produce steel efficiently. Jamsetji recognized that steel was not just an industrial product—it was the backbone of modern infrastructure, the key to building railroads, bridges, and factories. He realized that the absence of a robust steel industry in India was a huge disadvantage for the country's industrial and economic development.

The Vision for Tata Steel

Jamsetji's visionary idea was simple yet revolutionary for India at the time: he wanted to establish an indigenous steel industry in

India, which could make India self-sufficient and reduce its reliance on foreign imports. However, what made Jamsetji's idea so pioneering was his broader vision for self-reliance and nation-building through industrialization. His plan was not merely to produce steel; he envisaged an entire industrial ecosystem centered around it.

Drawing inspiration from what he saw in Pittsburgh, Jamsetji began to formulate his plans to build India's first steel plant. But unlike the steel plants in the West, Jamsetji's dream was intertwined with his belief in social progress. He wanted his steel plant to not only cater to the needs of industrialization but also contribute to the welfare of the Indian people. This was evident in the location of the plant: it was to be built in a region far from the metropolitan centers but in a way that it could serve as a hub for employment and community development.

Jamsetji's ambition extended beyond just industrial infrastructure. He dreamed of creating a township around the steel plant—a community where workers and their families would have access to education, healthcare, and sanitation. He imagined an integrated society where economic development went hand in hand with social welfare, a concept that was groundbreaking in a colonial India. His vision of Jamshedpur (named after him), which eventually became the site of Tata Steel, embodies this integrated approach to industrialization and welfare.

The challenge, however, was immense. Tata faced significant obstacles to making his dream a reality. India lacked the technology and know-how to produce steel on a large scale, and Jamsetji had to secure the right resources, including funding, skilled labor, and the appropriate site for the plant. He encountered skepticism from various quarters, particularly from colonial authorities who did not believe that an indigenous steel plant could succeed. Nevertheless, Jamsetji's determination and his trust in India's potential propelled him forward.

To secure the necessary capital, Jamsetji first sought out support from global investors. He was also able to attract a talented team of engineers and laborers, many of whom were brought from abroad, to develop the steel plant. He believed that India could be an industrial power if it had the right mix of visionary leadership, advanced technology, and national pride.

Jamsetji Tata passed away in 1904, long before his dream of Tata Steel came to fruition. However, his vision did not die with him. His successors, led by his son Sir Dorabji Tata, carried forward his dream. In 1907, the Tata Iron and Steel Company (TISCO) was established in Jamshedpur with the goal of producing steel for India's growing industrial needs.

Tata Steel began operations in 1912, and over time, it not only met the industrial needs of the country but also helped India achieve greater industrial independence. The city of Jamshedpur, once a barren landscape, transformed into an industrial powerhouse, and Tata Steel became a symbol of India's industrial revolution.

Jamsetji Tata's commitment to nation-building through industrialization led him to develop the first steel plant in India, as well as other monumental contributions. His other ventures included the creation of Indian Institute of Science (IISc) in Bangalore, and he also laid the groundwork for the Tata Power company, which became one of India's first power-generation companies.

(Henry Ford)-

In the late 19th century, Ford worked as an engineer at the Edison Illuminating Company in Detroit. This job not only provided him with a steady income but also connected him with the network of engineers and business minds of the era, including the legendary inventor Thomas Edison himself. During his time with the company, Ford's inventive spirit grew, and he spent his spare hours working on his own mechanical projects, often late into the night. These experiences fueled his determination to create a vehicle that could transform the way people lived and traveled.

However, the moment that set the course for Ford's revolutionary approach to automobile manufacturing came during his visit to the meatpacking plants in Chicago. At the time, the meatpacking industry was known for employing a method called the disassembly line, where animal carcasses were moved along a conveyor belt, and each worker had a specific task to perform, such as cutting or processing. The process was efficient and allowed the company to break down an animal quickly and in a systematic manner, ensuring high productivity and minimal waste. Ford observed this operation with fascination, noting how workers stayed stationary while the product moved, each performing a simple, repetitive task.

Ford's inventive mind immediately began to connect the dots. If this systematic approach could streamline the process of disassembling, could the same principle be applied in reverse to assemble products? The key insight he gleaned was that breaking down complex processes into simpler, smaller steps would allow for specialization, faster production, and reduced costs. It was this profound realization that laid the foundation for Ford's later development of the moving assembly line.

By the early 1900s, Ford was already working on building automobiles, having founded the Ford Motor Company in 1903.

His first major success was the Model A, but it was with the Model T, introduced in 1908, that he truly envisioned democratizing car ownership. The Model T was designed to be simple, affordable, and reliable, embodying Ford's belief that every American should have access to personal transportation. Yet, the traditional methods of car manufacturing were labor-intensive and time-consuming, making cars expensive and limiting their reach to the affluent.

Determined to change this, Ford revisited the idea inspired by the meatpacking disassembly line. In 1913, he implemented the world's first moving assembly line at his Highland Park factory in Michigan. The process involved a conveyor system that brought the vehicle chassis to the workers, each of whom performed a single, repetitive task. This was revolutionary because it minimized the movement required by the workers, significantly increased efficiency, and reduced the time it took to produce a car. What once took over 12 hours to assemble could now be completed in just 90 minutes.

The impact of this innovation was immediate and profound. Ford's assembly line not only sped up production but also lowered costs, enabling him to reduce the price of the Model T. Initially priced at $825, the price dropped to as low as $260 by the 1920s, making car ownership attainable for a much larger segment of the population. The Model T became a sensation, selling millions of units and cementing Ford's reputation as a visionary leader in the automotive world.

Beyond making cars affordable, Ford's use of the assembly line had a ripple effect throughout the industrial sector. The efficiency of mass production that Ford pioneered became known as "Fordism," which combined large-scale manufacturing with high wages for workers. Ford's decision to pay his employees a then-unheard-of wage of $5 a day in 1914 was both a moral and strategic move; it helped reduce turnover, motivated workers, and allowed them to become customers of the products they built. This move demonstrated Ford's forward-thinking approach, understanding that a prosperous workforce was integral to sustaining growth and expanding the consumer base.

Ford's approach revolutionized manufacturing, not just in the automobile industry but in industries worldwide. Factories began to adopt and adapt Ford's methods, ushering in an era of mass production and changing the landscape of manufacturing forever. His system of dividing labor into highly specialized tasks laid the groundwork for modern assembly lines seen in various industries today, from electronics to food production.

The success of the assembly line and the widespread adoption of the Model T solidified Ford's position as one of the greatest industrialists in history. The Ford Motor Company expanded rapidly, becoming a major global corporation. The Model T was not just a car; it symbolized freedom and innovation and represented a shift in society where mobility became accessible to the masses. The sheer scale of Ford's production led to significant advancements in logistics and supply chain management, with Ford developing large, integrated plants and securing raw materials to streamline production.

Ford's legacy extended far beyond the tangible impact of his automobiles. His vision set the stage for the automobile becoming a central feature of modern life, influencing urban planning, road infrastructure, and lifestyle. The Ford Motor Company continued to innovate, producing more models and adapting to changing markets, but it was the fundamental shift that Henry Ford initiated that transformed the industry and earned him a lasting place in history.

Henry Ford's story of innovation and relentless pursuit of efficiency remains a testament to the power of observing, learning, and reimagining existing processes to create something revolutionary. His experience at the Chicago meatpacking plants, which sparked his groundbreaking idea, illustrates the importance of cross-industry inspiration and how unconventional thinking can lead to transformative success.

(John D. Rockefeller)-

John D. Rockefeller's journey to becoming one of the most powerful and influential figures in American business history is marked by a series of decisive and pivotal moments. Among these, one of the most defining incidents that sparked Rockefeller's vision for the creation of Standard Oil was his deep insight into the burgeoning oil industry and his innovative approach to business that laid the foundation for modern corporate structures.

In the mid-19th century, Rockefeller was raised in a modest household in Richford, New York, and later in Cleveland, Ohio. His early life was shaped by a combination of his father's shrewd, albeit morally questionable, business tactics and his mother's piety and discipline. From a young age, Rockefeller displayed a keen sense for business and finance, often lending small sums of money to neighbors at a profit. This early acumen and interest in managing resources and capital would play a crucial role in his later success.

The turning point for Rockefeller came in the early 1860s during the Pennsylvania oil boom. At that time, crude oil was discovered in Titusville, Pennsylvania, sparking a rush akin to the California Gold Rush. However, the industry was chaotic and unstable, with countless small drilling operations vying for dominance and lacking any semblance of standardization or organization. The volatile nature of oil production led to unpredictable supply chains and fluctuating prices.

Rockefeller, then working as a successful produce commission merchant in Cleveland, saw the potential of the oil industry not in drilling but in refining. He recognized that the real profits were to be made in refining crude oil into kerosene, which was used for lighting homes before the widespread adoption of electricity. This insight came at a time when most individuals were still focused on striking oil and extracting it, but Rockefeller foresaw the long-term benefits of controlling the refinement and distribution processes.

In 1863, Rockefeller, along with a few partners, invested in his first refinery in Cleveland. He meticulously studied the operations and quickly identified inefficiencies. One of the most notable challenges at the time was the wastefulness of the refining process, as byproducts such as gasoline were often discarded. Rockefeller's detail-oriented approach led to innovations that improved efficiency and minimized waste. He understood that by using every part of the crude oil and selling byproducts, the profitability of his operations would increase significantly.

The establishment of the Standard Oil Company in 1870 marked the beginning of Rockefeller's systematic rise to dominance. Rockefeller implemented his strategic vision by focusing on vertical integration—owning not just the refineries but also the transportation and distribution networks. This allowed him to streamline operations, cut costs, and outmaneuver competitors. One of his most famous moves was negotiating with railroads for preferential rates, which greatly reduced his transportation expenses and put other refiners at a disadvantage. This tactic, though controversial, showcased Rockefeller's relentless drive to secure his position in the industry.

One of the key challenges Rockefeller faced during the early years of Standard Oil was the fierce competition and the public outcry over his business practices. Competitors accused him of employing unfair methods to dominate the market, such as undercutting prices to drive them out of business or buying them out at low prices. Despite these accusations, Rockefeller remained steadfast in his belief that consolidation and efficiency were necessary to stabilize the fledgling oil industry and ensure a consistent supply of kerosene to the masses.

Rockefeller's vision went beyond just profits; he sought to create an oil monopoly that would enable economies of scale. By the 1880s, Standard Oil controlled approximately 90% of the U.S. refining capacity, which effectively made Rockefeller a titan of the industry. His relentless pursuit of efficiency and dominance transformed the oil industry, leading to innovations such as pipelines to bypass railroads, which further reduced costs and solidified Standard Oil's market position.

As his empire grew, Rockefeller faced increasing scrutiny from the government and the public. The Sherman Antitrust Act of 1890 was a direct response to the monopoly practices of Standard Oil and other large trusts. Despite these challenges, Rockefeller managed to keep his company resilient, employing strategies such as forming trusts and reorganizing the company into various subsidiaries to maintain control while adapting to changing regulations.

Rockefeller's Legacy: Rockefeller's rise through the founding and expansion of Standard Oil set a precedent for modern business practices and corporate strategies. His ability to identify potential in an untapped market, innovate within that space, and execute his vision with unmatched precision marked a turning point in industrial capitalism. His efforts established him as the archetype of a self-made magnate, influencing the course of American and global business practices for generations.

(Andrew Carnegie)-

Andrew Carnegie's journey from a poor Scottish immigrant to the steel magnate who redefined American industry is a story marked by resilience, innovation, and an unwavering belief in the power of progress. His most transformative moment, which sparked his ambition to dominate the steel industry and shape modern infrastructure, came from a mix of personal determination and seizing the right opportunities at pivotal moments.

Carnegie was born in Dunfermline, Scotland, in 1835, to a family that faced economic hardship. His father was a weaver, but with the advent of mechanized looms, the family's livelihood was threatened. Seeking a better life, they immigrated to the United States in 1848, settling in Allegheny, Pennsylvania. Carnegie's early years in America were marked by long hours of work to help support his family. He started as a bobbin boy in a cotton factory and later became a telegraph messenger, learning the intricacies of communication and business.

A turning point in Carnegie's life came when he secured a job as a personal assistant to Thomas A. Scott, a superintendent at the Pennsylvania Railroad Company. This position exposed Carnegie to the vast potential of the railway system and the broader logistics and industrial sectors. Under Scott's mentorship, Carnegie learned the value of investment and strategic thinking. He began investing in small ventures, including iron bridges and rail companies, which brought him substantial returns and the confidence to pursue larger endeavors.

The spark for Carnegie's entry into the steel industry came during the 1850s and 1860s, when the need for stronger and more durable construction materials grew due to the expansion of the railway system and urban development. Carnegie witnessed firsthand the inefficiencies of the iron industry and recognized that steel, with its superior strength and flexibility, would be the material of the future. However, at the time, steel production was expensive and time-consuming.

In 1872, during a visit to England, Carnegie learned about the Bessemer process, a new method for producing steel that was far more efficient than traditional techniques. The process, invented by Henry Bessemer, allowed for the mass production of steel at a significantly reduced cost. Realizing the transformative potential of this method, Carnegie decided to bring it back to the United States and establish a steel empire.

By 1875, he opened the Edgar Thomson Steel Works near Pittsburgh, named after the president of the Pennsylvania Railroad. This move marked the birth of his steel empire. Carnegie's focus on innovation, cost-cutting, and reinvestment of profits set his company apart. He adopted vertical integration strategies, controlling every aspect of production, from the raw materials to transportation and manufacturing. This strategy not only improved efficiency but also allowed him to outcompete and outprice his rivals.

Challenges were not absent from Carnegie's journey. The steel industry was notorious for harsh labor conditions, and his factories were no exception. Carnegie's focus on maximizing productivity often led to long hours and dangerous working environments for his employees. This focus on efficiency culminated in the infamous Homestead Strike of 1892, where a violent labor dispute at the Homestead Steel Plant erupted between striking workers and company-hired security. Though Carnegie was abroad during the strike, the event left a lasting mark on his legacy, illustrating the tension between his business practices and public perception.

Carnegie's empire ultimately paved the way for the construction of skyscrapers, railroads, and bridges that defined American infrastructure. His ability to foresee the industrial needs of the country, combined with his relentless pursuit of innovation, made him one of the most influential business leaders of the Gilded Age.

Carnegie sold Carnegie Steel Company to J.P. Morgan in 1901 for $480 million, making it the largest industrial transaction of its time and giving rise to the United States Steel Corporation. Carnegie's fortune was vast, but his later life was defined by his commitment to philanthropy. He believed in the principle that "the man who dies rich dies disgraced," leading him to donate most of his wealth to educational, cultural, and scientific institutions, including the establishment of Carnegie Hall and countless public libraries across the U.S.

Carnegie passed away in 1919, but his legacy endures through his contributions to both industry and society, showcasing his belief in progress, innovation, and the responsibilities of wealth.

(Walt Disney)-

Walt Disney's journey from a small-town artist to the founder of a global entertainment empire is a tale of vision, resilience, and unmatched creativity. His most pivotal moment came not from a single spark, but from a series of challenges and breakthroughs that cemented his status as a pioneer in animation and storytelling.

Born on December 5, 1901, in Chicago, Illinois, Walt Disney grew up in a family that moved frequently due to his father's business ventures. His early years were marked by both struggle and imagination. Disney showed an interest in art from a young age, often selling sketches to neighbors and friends. When the family moved to Marceline, Missouri, Walt's love for storytelling blossomed amid the rural scenery and small-town charm, elements that would later inspire his work.

By the time he was a teenager, the Disney family had moved to Kansas City, where Walt attended McKinley High School and took evening classes at the Chicago Art Institute. After dropping out of high school to join the Red Cross Ambulance Corps during World War I, he spent time in France driving ambulances and drawing cartoons on the side of vehicles.

Walt returned to the United States determined to pursue a career in art and animation. In 1920, he began working at a small ad company where he met Ub Iwerks, an animator who would become an essential creative partner. Together, they opened Laugh-O-Gram Studios, an early animation venture that produced short films. However, despite their innovative ideas, Laugh-O-Gram faced severe financial difficulties and eventually went bankrupt. This setback, while disheartening, didn't deter Disney's ambition. Instead, it fueled his resolve to create something bigger.

In 1923, with only $40 in his pocket and a borrowed suitcase, Disney moved to Hollywood, where he founded the Disney Brothers Studio with his brother, Roy O. Disney. It was here that Walt's most significant breakthrough occurred. In 1928, after losing the rights to his first popular character, Oswald the Lucky Rabbit, to a rival studio, Disney was determined to create a character that he would own entirely. On a train ride back to California, he sketched the initial design for Mickey Mouse.

Mickey Mouse made his debut in the short film Steamboat Willie, which was one of the first animations to feature synchronized sound. The film was an immediate success, captivating audiences and setting the stage for Disney's unique approach to storytelling that combined art, technology, and music.

With Mickey's popularity soaring, Disney continued to push the boundaries of animation. In 1937, he released Snow White and the Seven Dwarfs, the world's first full-length animated feature film. Despite skepticism and being dubbed "Disney's Folly" by critics, Snow White's groundbreaking success at the box office cemented Disney's reputation as an industry innovator. It became the highest-grossing film of its time and demonstrated that animation could tell complex, emotional stories.

The 1940s and 1950s saw Disney expanding his studio's repertoire with classics like Pinocchio, Fantasia, Dumbo, and Bambi, each contributing to advances in animation techniques and storytelling. His next ambitious venture was creating a theme park that would bring stories to life. This vision materialized as Disneyland, which opened in 1955 in Anaheim, California. Unlike any amusement park before, Disneyland was meticulously designed to immerse visitors in Disney's beloved stories and characters, blending fantasy and reality.

However, success did not come without challenges. The development of Disneyland was financially risky, and Disney faced skepticism from investors and the media. He poured his personal funds into the project, demonstrating his unwavering commitment. Disneyland's immense success validated Disney's dream and laid the groundwork for future expansions, including Walt Disney World in Florida, though Disney would not live to see its completion.

Walt Disney's relentless pursuit of innovation extended into new technologies, such as pioneering the use of multiplane cameras to add depth to animation. His company also diversified into television with shows like The Mickey Mouse Club and Walt Disney's Wonderful World of Color, further solidifying its place in American culture.

Disney's influence continued to grow until his untimely death from lung cancer on December 15, 1966, at the age of 65. Though he passed away before many of his grand projects were completed, his legacy was carried forward by The Walt Disney Company, which expanded into global theme parks, a multitude of beloved films, and acquisitions of major franchises such as Pixar, Marvel, and Lucasfilm.

The rise of Walt Disney and his company is a testament to resilience, forward-thinking, and an unmatched dedication to storytelling. From humble beginnings to becoming a symbol of dreams and creativity, Disney's story embodies the essence of turning imagination into reality, influencing generations and forever changing the entertainment industry.

(Steve Jobs)-

Steve Jobs' life and career were marked by moments of sheer brilliance, groundbreaking innovation, and notable challenges that shaped his legacy as one of the most influential figures in technology. His journey from a young, ambitious entrepreneur to the co-founder of Apple Inc. and a leader in the tech world is a story of determination, creativity, and resilience.

Early Life and Spark of Interest in Technology Born on February 24, 1955, in San Francisco, California, Steve was adopted by Paul and Clara Jobs, who raised him in Mountain View—now part of Silicon Valley. Paul, a machinist, nurtured Jobs' early fascination with mechanics, teaching him how to take apart and reassemble electronics. This practical experience fostered an early appreciation for design and craftsmanship. Jobs' schooling was tumultuous; he was known for being a highly intelligent but rebellious student who often clashed with teachers and struggled with conventional education methods.

Despite these challenges, Jobs' curiosity led him to Hewlett-Packard (HP) meetings, where he encountered Steve Wozniak, a computer whiz with whom he shared a passion for electronics and computing. Jobs briefly attended Reed College in Oregon, where he explored interests in calligraphy and philosophy before dropping out after just one semester. This seemingly unimportant detour would later play a significant role in his design philosophies at Apple.

Founding of Apple and Early Challenges In 1976, Jobs and Wozniak co-founded Apple Computer in Jobs' garage, launching their first product, the Apple I. The duo combined Jobs' business acumen with Wozniak's engineering genius to create the Apple II, one of the first highly successful personal computers. It was a revolutionary machine that brought computing into homes, establishing Apple as a major player in the fledgling industry.

The company grew rapidly, and by 1984, Jobs introduced the Apple Macintosh. This computer was notable for its user-friendly graphical interface and innovative design, setting the standard for future PCs. However, internal conflicts at Apple began to escalate. Jobs' visionary but sometimes abrasive leadership style clashed with other executives, leading to power struggles. By 1985, after a contentious boardroom battle, Jobs resigned from Apple—a move that many thought would mark the end of his career in the tech industry.

The NeXT Chapter and Pixar Success Undeterred, Jobs founded NeXT Computer, focusing on creating high-end workstations for business and education. Though the NeXT computers were technologically advanced, they were commercially unsuccessful. However, NeXT's innovations would later prove essential, as its software formed the foundation for Apple's future operating systems.

Simultaneously, Jobs invested in Pixar Animation Studios, which had been a part of Lucasfilm's computer graphics division before he acquired it in 1986. Under Jobs' leadership, Pixar shifted from a niche hardware company to a powerhouse in animation. Its first film, Toy Story (1995), was the first-ever fully computer-animated feature film and a massive success. Pixar's groundbreaking storytelling and animation cemented Jobs' reputation as a visionary in both technology and entertainment.

Return to Apple and Unprecedented Success In 1996, Apple, struggling with dwindling market share and internal disarray, acquired NeXT, bringing Jobs back as an advisor and later as interim CEO. Jobs embarked on an ambitious turnaround plan that involved streamlining the product line, reinvigorating the company culture, and focusing on user-friendly design. The release of the iMac in 1998 marked a new era for Apple, featuring a unique, colorful design that attracted widespread consumer attention.

Jobs' tenure saw the introduction of iconic products that revolutionized technology and consumer electronics. The iPod (2001) changed the way people listened to music, while the iTunes Store transformed the music industry by offering digital downloads. In 2007, Jobs unveiled the iPhone, a revolutionary device that combined a phone, iPod, and internet browser, effectively launching the smartphone era. This was followed by the App Store in 2008, which created a new ecosystem for developers and expanded the device's capabilities exponentially.

Later Years and Legacy In 2010, Jobs introduced the iPad, which popularized the tablet market. His relentless pursuit of innovation and excellence positioned Apple as a leader in the tech industry. By this time, Apple had become one of the most valuable companies in the world, driven by Jobs' vision for creating products that blended technology with intuitive user experiences.

Despite his success, Jobs faced significant health challenges. He was diagnosed with a rare form of pancreatic cancer in 2004 and took several medical leaves over the years. On October 5, 2011, Jobs passed away at the age of 56, leaving behind an unmatched legacy in the tech industry. His impact extended beyond the products he created; Jobs redefined how technology interacts with everyday life, emphasizing the importance of design, simplicity, and innovation.

Today, Apple continues to build on his legacy with new products and technological advancements that echo Jobs' philosophy: "Stay hungry, stay foolish." His influence is evident in the way modern tech companies approach design, marketing, and product development, ensuring that Steve Jobs remains an enduring figure *in the story of technological progress.*

(Cornelius Vanderbilt)-

One of the key moments that propelled Cornelius Vanderbilt toward becoming a formidable figure in the transportation industry was his realization during the War of 1812. At that time, the United States was at war with Great Britain, which led to a significant disruption in trade and maritime activities. The British naval blockade stifled commerce along the American coast, creating a shortage of transportation options for people and goods.

Vanderbilt, then just a teenager, saw an opportunity in the chaos. Using a small boat he borrowed money to purchase, he began ferrying supplies and passengers between Staten Island and Manhattan. This venture proved highly profitable, as it met a critical need for movement during wartime when other shipping options were scarce or unreliable. Vanderbilt's operations, although small-scale at first, were efficient and cost-effective, earning him significant local recognition and financial success.

This early venture was crucial because it showcased Vanderbilt's innate ability to identify and exploit market gaps. He quickly gained a reputation for being reliable, hardworking, and fiercely competitive. The success of his ferrying business not only provided him with capital but also laid the groundwork for his future ventures in steamships and, eventually, railroads.

This wartime experience solidified Vanderbilt's understanding of the transportation sector and marked the beginning of his journey from a modest ferryman to the "Commodore," a title that would become synonymous with his dominance in the shipping and railroad industries. His early decision to act during the War of 1812 highlighted his foresight and risk-taking abilities, traits that would define his business career for decades to come.

(john Pierpont (J.P.) Morgan)-

John Pierpont (J.P.) Morgan, one of the most prominent and influential American financiers of the 19th and early 20th centuries, had a defining moment early in his life that sparked his business acumen and laid the foundation for his vast empire. One of the key incidents that catalyzed his rise in the world of finance occurred in 1857, when he was just 20 years old.

At that time, J.P. Morgan worked for his father's bank in New York City, J.P. Morgan & Co., a small but reputable financial institution. During this period, the Panic of 1857—a major economic depression—struck the United States, resulting in widespread bank failures, business bankruptcies, and a severe financial crisis. As the market collapsed, many businesses were left vulnerable to failure, and there was a significant loss of public confidence in the stability of the nation's financial system.

In the midst of the panic, J.P. Morgan's quick thinking and strategic actions would define his future success. His father, Junius Morgan, was a well-established banker with strong European ties, and this provided J.P. Morgan with important connections and insight into global financial systems. During the panic, when many other banks were in turmoil, Morgan played a pivotal role in stabilizing the market by helping to organize the reorganization of failing banks and facilitating the extension of credit to businesses on the brink of collapse.

One notable act during the panic involved Morgan's personal intervention to support New York's banks. The banks were about to face massive losses when several prominent firms faltered. In a move that would later define his career, J.P. Morgan took it upon himself to personally step in and save the banks. He used his own funds, combined with his family's assets, to reorganize and stabilize several banks, ensuring that they did not collapse. His bold actions prevented a complete financial disaster and cemented his reputation as a powerful financier capable of managing and stabilizing troubled financial systems.

This experience during the Panic of 1857 not only proved his financial brilliance but also showcased his risk-taking ability, leadership, and capacity to see opportunities in times of crisis. From this moment on, Morgan was seen as the go-to financier in moments of national financial uncertainty.

After the panic, J.P. Morgan continued to solidify his position as one of the leading financiers in America. He expanded his influence and grew his firm, eventually focusing on mergers and acquisitions, particularly in the railroad industry, where he would eventually amass a vast fortune by consolidating major railroads and ensuring their profitability. By the 1880s and 1890s, J.P. Morgan's wealth and influence reached unparalleled heights, and he became a key figure in the shaping of the modern American financial landscape.

J.P. Morgan's rise was marked by his ability to turn financial crises into opportunities, and his legacy endures as one of the most important figures in the development of global finance. His role in the creation of General Electric and the U.S. Steel Corporation—along with his influence in stabilizing the U.S. economy during several financial crises—earned him the title of "The King of Wall Street."

Through his decisive actions during the panic and subsequent years, J.P. Morgan's career helped shape the path of modern finance. He became synonymous with not just wealth, but the power of financial institutions and their ability to control the economic pulse of a nation

(Thomas Edison)-

The incident that sparked Thomas Edison's business journey and forever changed the world was his invention of the electric light bulb. However, it wasn't just the invention itself that was pivotal; it was the series of challenges and failures that led to his breakthrough and his unique approach to transforming that invention into a global business.

In the late 1870s, the world relied primarily on gas lamps for illumination. Edison, already an established inventor with a curiosity for solving practical problems, saw an opportunity to improve this outdated system. His business idea came when he realized that electric lighting could not only replace gas lamps but could be far more efficient and safer.

The specific incident that sparked his vision happened during his intense experimentation with various materials for the light bulb filament. By 1879, Edison and his team at his Menlo Park laboratory had already experimented with hundreds of materials, such as platinum and carbon, but none of them could withstand the heat and provide the necessary longevity for a practical electric light. Edison's eureka moment came when he discovered that carbonized bamboo worked as an effective filament. This discovery, which allowed the bulb to burn for more than 1200 hours, solved the critical problem of light bulb durability.

But Edison's insight wasn't just about inventing a working bulb. He realized that a light bulb on its own would be of little use unless he could create a reliable electrical distribution system to supply power to homes and businesses. He envisioned a world where electricity would replace gas as the main source of lighting, and this vision laid the foundation for his business empire.

What set Edison apart was his understanding that for his invention to have any significant impact, it needed to be scaled into a complete system. This meant designing not only the light bulb but also the infrastructure to generate and distribute electricity to power homes, factories, and streets. In 1882, Edison opened the world's first commercial power plant on Pearl Street in Manhattan. This was the birth of modern electric utilities, and it was a monumental step towards Edison's larger vision of electrifying cities worldwide.

A Business Empire: General Electric and Beyond

Edison didn't stop with the light bulb and electric utility systems. Over the years, his company, Edison General Electric, expanded rapidly. He went on to develop key innovations such as the phonograph and the motion picture camera, both of which would create entirely new industries. Edison was not just an inventor, but a savvy businessman, knowing how to commercialize his ideas, protect his intellectual property, and scale his business.

By the end of the 19th century, General Electric (GE), which was born from Edison's vision, became a global leader in electrical technology. His company diversified into home appliances, lighting, and even aviation technologies. Edison's business foresight and inventions created industries that continue to influence the world today.

(George Eastman)-

George Eastman's business journey and the rise of Eastman Kodak began with a crucial incident in his life—a moment that sparked his desire to revolutionize the photography industry and create a global enterprise that would make photography accessible to the masses.

In the late 19th century, photography was a complicated and expensive process. Early photography required bulky equipment, complex chemical processes, and professional knowledge, making it a privilege only for those with the right resources. George Eastman was an innovative thinker who believed that photography should be something everyone could do—an accessible hobby for the average person.

In 1877, Eastman had the pivotal insight that would change the industry. After experimenting with wet plate processes, Eastman realized that the process of developing photographs could be made simpler and more accessible if it was portable. The invention of a flexible, roll-film camera would be the key to revolutionizing photography.

The Key Incident: The Invention of the Kodak Camera

The most significant incident that sparked Eastman's rise was the creation of the Kodak camera in 1888. Eastman developed a camera that was small, portable, and, most importantly, used roll film. Prior to this, traditional photography relied on glass plates that were cumbersome and fragile. Eastman's innovation was groundbreaking—he used a flexible, light-sensitive film that could be easily rolled up, making it not only easier to use but also more durable.

But Eastman's breakthrough wasn't just in creating a portable camera. He understood that the camera alone wouldn't make photography mainstream. The real revolution came with his decision to offer customers preloaded film rolls that could be mailed back to Kodak for development. When customers were finished taking their pictures, they could simply send the film to Kodak, and Kodak would process it, print the photos, and return the developed images along with a fresh roll of film for the camera.

This model made photography accessible to everyday people. It eliminated the need for specialized knowledge and expensive equipment. The Kodak camera was easy to use, and the service Kodak provided was incredibly convenient, allowing amateur photographers to enjoy the experience without worrying about the technical complexities.

The success of the Kodak camera was immediate. With a simple slogan that read, "You press the button, we do the rest," Kodak made photography a common pastime. In just one year, Kodak sold over 100,000 cameras, each priced at just $25—a relatively affordable price at the time. Kodak's market was now the general public, not just professional photographers, and the company soon became the leading brand in the photographic industry.

Eastman's vision of making photography accessible to everyone wasn't just about selling cameras; it was about creating an entirely new way of capturing memories. The success of Kodak was a cultural transformation, as millions of people began using cameras to document their lives and personal experiences.

Eastman's business sense and entrepreneurial vision propelled Kodak into becoming a dominant force in the photography industry. As demand grew, Kodak expanded its product line to include not only cameras and film but also photographic paper *and other related accessories.*

Eastman's marketing genius was instrumental in building Kodak's global brand. He used aggressive advertising and innovative distribution techniques to ensure Kodak was available everywhere. Kodak's growth was so rapid that by the late 1890s, the company had a global presence, opening manufacturing plants and sales offices worldwide.

But Kodak's innovation didn't stop with the invention of the camera and film. Eastman led the company into new areas, developing products like Kodachrome, a color film that became widely popular and was essential in creating the foundation for modern color photography. Eastman's ability to create new products and market them effectively turned Kodak into one of the most influential companies in the world by the early 20th century.

Signature Collection

Ratan Tata Note- Jamsetji Nusserwanji Tata's signature not
available

Henry Ford

John D. Rockefeller

Andreew Carnegie

Walt Disney

Steve Jobs

Cornelius Vanderbilt

john Pierpont (J.P.) Morgan

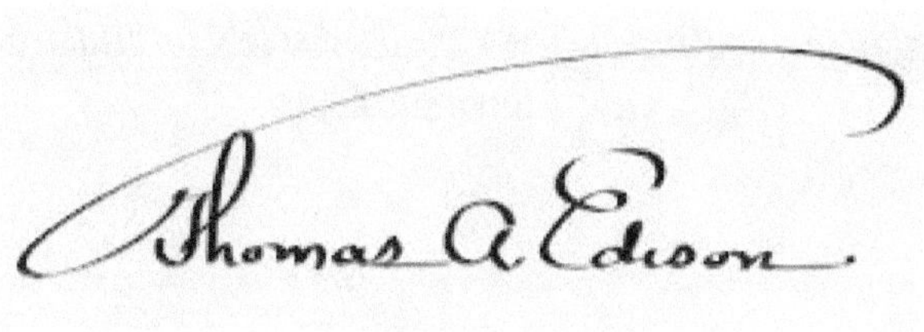

Thomas edision

George Eastman

Authors Autobiography

My name is Adeeb Jamal, and I am currently in the 11th grade at Allenhouse Public School, located in Khalasi Line, Kanpur. From a young age, I have been deeply curious about the intersection of technology, business, and innovation. My passion for these fields led me to pursue research on cutting-edge topics, which I have shared through multiple research papers published in renowned journals like IRJET, IRJMETS, and IJPREMS.

In addition to my academic pursuits, I have sought to expand my knowledge through various online courses, completing several high-level programs on platforms like Coursera. These courses span areas such as quantum computing, cybersecurity, project management, and business analytics. These courses have helped me develop a deeper understanding of the modern business world and the technological advancements shaping it.

Alongside my studies, I have been involved in a number of professional projects, including hands-on work with Microsoft Sentinel, Azure Active Directory, and robotics engineering. These projects have allowed me to apply theoretical knowledge in practical scenarios, providing valuable insights into the technological side of business operations.

This book, Titans of Trade and Power, provides me with an opportunity to contribute to the understanding of influential business leaders and their legacies. While my academic journey is ongoing, my growing interest in business studies, AI, and their application to modern enterprises drives my ambition to explore how technology shapes the global business landscape. Through this work, I hope to offer my perspective on how we can leverage emerging technologies to create new avenues for growth and innovation in the business world.

Sources For The Book

Books on Business Icons

Taraporevala, R. (1995). Jamsetji Nusserwanji Tata: A Chronicle of His Vision and Legacy. Tata Press.

Chernow, R. (1998). Titan: The Life of John D. Rockefeller, Sr. Random House.

Nasaw, D. (2006). Andrew Carnegie. Penguin Books.

Gabler, N. (2006). Walt Disney: The Triumph of the American Imagination. Vintage.

Brinkley, D. (2003). Wheels for the World: Henry Ford, His Company, and a Century of Progress. Viking Adult.

Books on Tech Revolutionaries

Isaacson, W. (2011). Steve Jobs. Simon & Schuster.

Stiles, T. J. (2009). The First Tycoon: The Epic Life of Cornelius Vanderbilt. Vintage.

Strouse, J. (1999). Morgan: American Financier. Harper Perennial.

Baldwin, N. (1995). Edison: Inventing the Century. University of Chicago Press.

Books on Industry Visionaries

Brayer, E. (1996). George Eastman: A Biography. Johns Hopkins University Press.

Academic Articles and Journals

Ghemawat, P. (2016). "Jamsetji Tata and the Birth of Indian Industry." Harvard Business Review.

Lipartito, K. (2000). "The Impact of Rockefeller and Standard Oil on Modern Capitalism." Business History Review.

Historical Business Accounts

Chandler, A. D. (1990). Scale and Scope: The Dynamics of Industrial Capitalism. Belknap Press.
Schumpeter, J. A. (1942). Capitalism, Socialism, and Democracy. Harper & Brothers.

Autobiographies and Memoirs

Ford, H. (1922). My Life and Work. Doubleday, Page & Co.
Rockefeller, J. D. (1909). Random Reminiscences of Men and Events. Doubleday, Page & Co.

Historical Archives and Case Studies

Edison Papers Project (Rutgers University). The Thomas Edison Papers.
Morgan Library and Museum. J.P. Morgan Personal Archives.

Documentaries and Interviews

PBS (2000). The Men Who Built America.
National Geographic. Genius: Steve Jobs.

Magazines and Online Resources

"The Legacy of Jamsetji Tata," The Economic Times, Special Edition, 2018.
"100 Most Influential People in Business History," Forbes, 2015.
Biography.com profiles on Rockefeller, Carnegie, and Disney.

Collections and Signature Compilations

Wikipedia (Google Search)